Taking the Long Way Home

by

Robert A. Dolman

Dedicated to:

Our precious grandchildren Joshua, Elijah, Caleb, Seth and Sarah. Always remember that our love for you is unconditional.

Special thanks to Tanis Dolman-Johnson, John and Rosemary Rowlands and my wife Gail, for their assistance in editing this manuscript.

Contents

Introduction

I never knew my grandfather or my grandmother – both died when I was very young. At some point they immigrated to Canada from the Jersey Islands off the coast of France. Frank DeGruchy was a Frenchman, short and somewhat frail looking, yet I suspect much more a man than my worn photograph portrays. I still vaguely remember sitting with my mother at his bedside as he passed away. I was probably three or four years old at the time. I do know that he served Canada in the First World War, a proud member of the Royal Canadian Horse Artillery Regiment. Our family still retains his campaign medals, yet sadly, not much additional information concerning his exploits or adventures.

My grandmother's name was Florence. Her photograph portrays a heavy-set, motherly looking woman with the soft, warm eyes that seem to urge any hurting child to climb upon her knee. My knowledge of her is even more limited than that of my grandfather.

I wish Frank and Florence had lived longer, at least long enough to teach me French, or share some of the lessons they had learned on their life's journey. Why is it that we know so little of the significant people in our past? What a shame that so few took the time to record even the mundane events of their walk that we might have grasped something of what they struggled with, came to believe in, and valued in life, a wealth of experience and expertise blown away by the winds of time.

So it is exactly for this reason that I now take pen in hand to record some of the events that shaped and fashioned my own life perchance that someone may, through that which I relate, gain a valuable life lesson without the tragic necessity of having to experience the reality of it for themselves.

In recording these events, I have, in some instances, refrained from using *real names*; others are, of course, genuine and immediately recognizable. Even so, as I approach this task, I am reminded of a Chinese friend, Norman Jeng, who in producing a new menu for his restaurant included the names of a number of his regular customers on the front cover. What a mistake! Although he merely intended to thank a few loyal patrons many regular customers were offended that their names had not been included. Like Norman, I too have mentioned only a few people by name, and yet my intent is not to purposely avoid or overlook anyone who significantly influenced my life. I trust therefore that those friends and family who read this book and are not specifically mentioned will not be offended but will recognize immediately where in the context of this treatise their relationship impacted my life. To each of you I extend my heartfelt thanks for your contribution to my journey. May God bless you as you read it.

1
Prelude to Perdition

When my eyes began to focus, I realized I was lying on my back staring up at a street light. It was deathly quiet. Something was wrong. Something was missing – my friends – they were gone and I was alone. Slowly, it came back to me. We had been drinking – playing an imaginary game of football on a back street near the Victory Tea Room where our teenage gang hung out. I remember now. I had tried to tackle Norris, but he had simply stepped aside and allowed the telephone pole, concealed behind him, to absorb the impact. I hit that pole *head down* and at *full speed* and I fell to the street like a bundle of newspapers tossed from a passing truck.

But where was everybody now? It was about eleven o'clock in the evening when we left the tea room to play our fantasy football game. Maybe even now they were hiding in the shrubbery of the nearby houses, desperately trying to conceal their presence and their laughter. But my search was futile. There was no one in the bushes, no traffic on the street, no one in sight. My friends were gone. I was alone.

At a snail's pace I made my way back to the tea room. It was closed. I peered through the dirty window. The *Coca-cola clock* on the wall above the lunch counter broadcast the time – it was 3:30 – 3:30 A.M. My *good buddies* had left me lying there – *unconscious* on the street – apparently for more than four hours. Gingerly, I massaged the bump on my head, and started to walk the fifteen blocks home. It was too late now and far too dangerous to take the short cut across the railway tracks, wisely, I began *taking the long way home*.

2
Childhood Choices

Agatha Christie once wrote,

One of the luckiest things that can happen to you in life is, I think, to have a happy childhood.[1]

When I read her statement my first reaction was, *Well, I guess that let's me off the hook!* I supposed that since my childhood wasn't that *happy*, I could easily use it as an excuse to justify every form of failure in my life. After all, none of this was really *my fault.* And how many times since have I witnessed that long procession of people doing exactly that – blaming everything and everyone for their own failures? Anyway, who was it that ever said life was supposed to be fair?

But the fact is that my childhood wasn't all sunshine and lollipops. My father, Slim, was a well-known local country music entertainer with a small band that traveled extensively. He fought and drank his way through half the province of Saskatchewan and while he did, my mother, Joan, labored carrying fur coats at Eaton's Department store to provide the thirty-five dollars a

---

1 http://education.yahoo.com/reference/quotations/category/Child

month we needed for rent in order to keep a roof over our heads. Dad made money of course, but it seemed mom never saw much of it, and when necessities were needed, it was always mom who pulled out her little black change purse and anted up.

The house we lived in on twelve block Albert Street, in the city of Regina, was no prize. The walls weren't insulated. There was no furnace. The only heat came from a cook stove in the kitchen that mom would stoke up each night to see us through those bitterly cold Canadian winters. When nights were particularly cold she would put two *bricks* in the oven, one for my older sister Diane, and one for me. When they were sufficiently hot she'd wrap each brick in a towel and place them in our beds to keep us warm until we fell asleep. Some mornings we'd see frost on the inside of the walls. But mom's love kept that place warm on the coldest nights – nights when the long johns she brought in from the clothes line would stand at attention in the corner of the kitchen.

There was just a toilet in the bathroom, no shower, not even a sink. Washing-up was done from a basin in the kitchen. There was a portable galvanized bathtub that leaned against the wall in the back porch, but that porch was far too cold most of the time and a bath was a special treat – a right of springtime or a time for lingering reflection on a warm summer's night.

A trap door in the middle of the kitchen floor opened to reveal a small dirt dugout that was used for cold storage. A handful of preserves lined the wooden shelves on either side of the steep staircase. Altogether that old house wasn't much of a place to call home, but it was all we had and all we could afford and my sister Diane and I did what we could to help mom. Diane helped with the inside chores while I was charged with chopping wood and breaking up blocks of coal for the cookstove.

The coal shed in the back yard was made of galvanized tin and I spent many a cold winter's night chipping away at the large blocks of coal periodically delivered there. To this day I still marvel that I never lost an eye to one of those flying coal chips that regularly flew up and stung me. The sharp side of the axe was for chopping wood, the flat side for breaking up coal. Neither performed its function very efficiently.

On cold winter nights I found myself envying the few *rich kids* I knew whose families had homes with furnaces in the basement and whose coal deliveries came in the form of small nuggets instead of the blocks I was forced to struggle with. Those nuggets were funneled right down a window into their basement, and all a person had to do was shovel it directly into the furnace. Now that was bounty for you!

When dad did come home an argument was certain to ensue. Mom was practical and security conscious, dad was anything but, and when he was drinking, *reason* was his first victim. Some of that which took place was not very pleasant, but its resurrection today is of little importance, suffice, to say, I suppose, that on some particularly violent occasions, had I been able to lay my hand upon the means, I no doubt would have tried to take his life and when a child lies in bed on Christmas Eve praying that his father *would not come home*, that fact tells its own sad tale.

But in dad's defense he had not been the product of a particularly easy life himself. Growing up in England his mother died when he was but a small lad and his stepmother was less than tolerant of her ready-made family. He had come to Canada on the *Empress of Britain*, earning his passage as a singer in the nightly dinner show. When he couldn't find a job he bought himself a cheap guitar, walked into a local radio station and said he was there to audition as a *singing cowboy*. He sang two songs and was hired on the spot – six days a week, for a full two dollars weekly. They told him to be back to start the next morning. He left the station and decided he had better learn some more cowboy songs since he had used the only two he knew in the audition. Remarkably, his talent allowed him to perform on local radio stations for more than twenty years and he was eventually inducted into the country music hall of fame under his radio name of *Slim Wilson*. I guess Cyril George John Isaac Dolman just doesn't cut it for a cowboy singer. But whatever else might be said about him – *my dad sure could sing.*

But just like me my dad had no training in parenthood. Strange isn't it that you need a license to own a dog, or drive an automobile, but nothing to be a parent? Perhaps that's why so many of us go through life faking it and flying by the seat of our pants. Well, dad was no exception. He tried, but unfortunately, he had lived in England during an era when it was frowned upon, even considered unmanly, for fathers to show emotion or affection towards their children. A father might, well say, *Good Morning,* but a warm smile was seldom to be offered and a hug was out of the question.

So childhood for me was not a particularly *happy* time. There were no holidays and no efforts to encourage participation in any sports, clubs or outside activities, and although I did manage to join Cubs and Air Cadets, it was usually through my own initiative. Mom occasionally attended one of those functions and was always extremely proud of my every accomplishment, but dad was no where to be seen. There were no rides *to or from* and generally speaking very little parental support; although mom always made sure I had a clean shirt, a well pressed uniform and clean underwear – *just in case I might be involved in an accident.*

Sometimes on Sunday morning, if dad had come home late Saturday night, Diane and I would be shuffled off to a nearby Salvation Army Sunday school – probably more intended to get us out of the house than to provide us with any particular spiritual enlightenment. Yet mom always seemed to have a soft spot in her heart reserved for God. She was truly what one might call a *kindred spirit.* The Salvation Army Church on 7th Avenue was a warm and friendly place. They had a big bass drum which kids got to play during the singing portion of the service and thankfully every one of us got our turn. The accompanying trumpet and piano covered the invariable blunders of that child-like percussion section as we sounded out old gospel favorites like *Power in the Blood* and *The Old Rugged Cross.* We truly rocked that little chapel on Sunday mornings.

Diane and I didn't attend that little Sally-Ann chapel for very long, but we did linger long enough to go with them on the train to Regina Beach for the annual Sunday school picnic. It was my first train ride and it was a true adventure. But one event marred the proceedings – when I went to eat my brown paper bagged lunch I discovered the ants had gotten into it. Then, as I sat there crying, a Salvation Army lady came, sat down beside me and gave me her own. I hope one day in heaven I can thank her. Our days in Sunday school were short but I never forget the love and kindness displayed to us by the men and women who wore those blue and red uniforms and I was confident of one thing – if I ever needed a meal I could always turn to them.

So it was with a great deal of pride that one day I brought home a picture Bible with an inscription inside announcing that it had been awarded to me for the *highest marks in the primary Sunday School Class.* Little did I realize then how I would pack that Bible with me from pillar to post for the rest of my life, nor how one day it would play an instrumental role in preserving my life. It was a *trophy*, my first real prize, and I cherished it.

Regular schooling for me began at Lorne School, an honest-to-God, *one room school house.* The only teacher, Miss Kelly, taught all the grades from kindergarten to grade three and I suppose, if nothing else, we learned the *principle of osmosis* first hand, because we couldn't help but absorb some of what was taught to the older students as we quietly completed our own assignments. But I also learned another important lesson at Lorne School – teachers expected children not to speak unless they were spoken to. It was my first and only run in with Miss Kelly and my first exposure to the dreaded razor strap. But I can tell you one thing – *I never spoke out of turn in class again.* It was grade one and although I didn't agree with the punishment, I never crossed Miss Kelly again. Whoever said that punishment was not a deterrent didn't know what they were talking about.

But there was another day in Lorne School I shall never forget. It was the day I heard one of the girls scream and someone holler, *Fire!* Surprisingly, it was no false alarm – our little red school house was suddenly ablaze and as we all began to panic, Miss Kelly stood at the front of the class like a member of the Royal Grenadier Guards and calmly ordered us to stay in our seats. The girls began to cry – the boys wished they could – flames licked up from every heat register in the classroom – smoke began to fill the building – and Miss Kelly marched us out one by one like so many toy soldiers on parade. Miss Kelly was the last one out the door, she was my hero and despite the fact that she had given me the strap, I loved her. I'm sure she was probably as frightened as we were but she was an old fashioned schoolmarm and would no doubt have given her life for any one of us. Of course there was a wonderful upside to the whole affair

– it took three months to repair the damage and it made for a wonderfully extended Christmas holiday.

With the school fire something that at first blush appeared *bad* ultimately turned into something *good*, but shortly afterwards something that appeared *good* had the opposite effect and turned into something *bad*. Someone decided I should skip grade two and be promoted from grade one directly into grade three. It was a decision that would haunt me throughout the remainder of my schooling. It not only made me the youngest student in every succeeding class but also caused me to fail to solidify some very fundamental mathematical skills from which I never seemed to adequately recover. I guess sometimes a little maturity can be gained even in grade two.

All too soon, however, those even mildly joyful days of early childhood were gone and I found myself a teenager, with a lack of any serious parental supervision, roaming the streets late at night, hanging around the Victory Tea Room, a Chinese restaurant on Dewdney Avenue, in the city of Regina, Saskatchewan, with my buddies Harold Reid and Bill Short. Harold was the strong, quiet type who soon moved away to Manitoba and like so many good friends over the course of one's life – just seemed to drift away. Who would ever have thought that one day, some forty years later, we'd be reunited through something called the *internet*?

Bill, on the other hand, was a dark complexioned man, man with a flattened face and mean look. Bill was a boxing champion whom someone had nicknamed the *Brown Bomber* and nobody, but nobody, messed with him. He endured open heart surgery before he was twenty, became an alcoholic, married, fathered a child, divorced and then quit drinking.

Bill was a real character who willingly admitted, after his open-heart surgery, that he could no longer play poker as well as he once did saying,

When the game gets quiet, everyone can hear the rhythm of my heart and they know if I have a good hand.

But he also confessed that his pacemaker came in handy when his young son reclined on his chest as he rocked him to sleep at night.

Bill's mother treated me like a son and mine treated Bill in the same way. Our mothers also shared some mutual marital hardships that bonded them in close friendship. Grenfell was Bill's dad. He was a hard drinker and Bill was often frustrated with him in the same way I was frustrated with my own father. But even then sometimes humor rounded off the sharp edges of conflict, like the night soon after I got my first car, when Bill asked if we could pick up his dad and bring him home from the beer parlour. Bill was furious with Grenfell that night and as we drove past the Molson's Brewery on Albert Street in the north end of Regina, Bill turned to his dad in the back seat and angrily said,

Do you see that place; they can make more beer than you can drink!

And in his drunken stupor, his dad simply smiled and said,

Yeah, but I got 'em working nights!

Tragically, Bill died before he turned thirty, when his vehicle collided with a semi-trailer truck late one night as he returned to his home in Estevan, Saskatchewan. Bill was like my brother and more than fifty years later I still miss him.

The warehouse district in which we lived was our kingdom and we knew every nook and cranny like the back of our hands. The loading docks, railroad spurs, back alleys and darkened doorways were our domain. I walked those streets tirelessly, night after night, first with Harold and later with Bill. Bill and I had a lot in common including fathers who were less than perfect role models. We were fourteen years old and on a serious downward spiral.

During the 1950's street gangs in the city of Regina were as common as they are in many major cities today. Thankfully, drugs were not a major issue and the disputes were settled with fists and occasionally switch blades. Today such differences are more often settled with guns. But the only gun incident concerning gangs in those days in Regina was when a store owner, tired of the constant trouble from gang members, pulled a shotgun from under his counter and killed a member of a gang known as the Lancers. The shopkeeper was charged with murder but subsequently acquitted and all shopkeepers soon began to put shotguns under their counters. Not surprisingly, within a few months you couldn't find a Lancer's jacket anywhere in the entire city.

But our group was more just a nuisance than any dangerous brotherhood of criminals and while we did our share of drinking we never engaged in any really serious criminal activity. We hung out around a place called the Victory Tea Room on Dewdney Avenue and we were really a mixed breed. Some from troubled homes, some from good homes; some would end up breaking the law and going to jail while others, like me, would ultimately end up working on the side of the law sending people to jail. We were teenagers; it was the 1950's, a time of rock-n-roll and rebellion and we were rocking, rolling and rebelling with the best of them.

3
High School Heroes

I don't know why it is that the most negative events in one's life sometimes bring the greatest blessing, but one of those negative incidents in my life was a decision by bureaucrats in the Regina Public School Board to draw a boundary line down the center of my street. That decision kept me from attending Scott Collegiate with my friends and forced me to travel eight miles by city transit bus to Balfour Technical Collegiate in the East end of Regina. It was to become one of the ironies of my life and I can still recall the intense anger I felt as I watched my friends walking just ten blocks to Scott while I stood waiting for a bus.

Balfour was more than twice the size of Scott Collegiate and filled with people from the North-East end of Regina. It was primarily a *technical* school and I was anything but a carpenter, electrician or a handyman, although there have been many times since when I wished I had been smart enough to become a plumber. Balfour was known as a *tough* school and although I had always fashioned myself a *hard rock,* I soon found that this school was filled with those who could make short work of a punk like me. It took me just one day at Balfour to remember the lesson Miss Kelly initially taught me so many years before – *to keep my mouth shut.*

Even the teachers at Balfour were tough and I often watched in awe as Mr. McKenzie, the vice principal, slammed a student up against the lockers to get his attention or reinforce a point of order. On one occasion, when our grade ten all-boys class sent the music teacher from the room in tears, Mr. McKenzie was the first to arrive on the scene. His first word was *Freeze!* And we all froze instantly to our chairs. Clarence Bittel moved. An enraged McKenzie threw aside six or seven chairs to get to him and when he did he made his point. I suppose an old cowboy would say, *He read to him from the book.* A teacher that acted like that today would find himself not only in court, but probably in jail. Not surprisingly, however, Mr. McKenzie never seemed to bother any student one might consider *truly dangerous*, and no student at Balfour was more dangerous than Tony Rapushka.

Tony carried a reputation that extended far beyond Balfour's hallways and made him one the most feared hoodlums in the city. His quickness and cat-like reflexes made him a street fighter to be avoided at all costs. In fact, with one swift upper cut, Tony could actually hit you four times. First, his fist would hit you in the stomach and with one upward, sweeping motion move on to contact your chin. By the time his fist hit your chin, his elbow was hitting your stomach. Then his elbow would follow through in exactly the same manner to your chin. I learned about that move in person when he hit me just that way and sprawled me against my locker. Tony was indeed a scary guy. Everybody knew Tony and purposefully gave him a wide berth. But one day Tony met his match in a not so scary looking history teacher by the name of Gordon Currie.

On the day it happened I was in my assigned seat directly behind Tony and Mr. Currie was teaching a history lesson from the front of the class. It was Spring and the sun's warm rays were streaming in through the windows that bordered one side of our classroom. It was one of those days when no one wanted to be there – not the students and not the teachers. The sun was clearly bothering Mr. Currie and rather than continue to shade his eyes from it he walked over to the window and pulled down the blind, effectively cutting the rays to the front of the classroom. Then he returned to his former position and continued to teach the lesson.

Tony apparently preferred the sunshine, for no sooner had Mr. Currie gotten to the front of the room than Tony stood up, walked over to the window, grabbed the O-ring of the blind and snapped it. Instantly the blind recoiled. Casually, he sauntered back to his seat and sat down. Without missing a word in the lesson Mr. Currie walked back to the window slowly pulled down the blind and returned again to the front of the class. You guessed it – Tony got up, slouched his way back to the window, flipped up the blind again and returned to his seat. Although the lesson continued the only sound that registered in anyone's mind was the whirling of that blind.

Then, methodically, Mr. Currie removed his suit jacket, hung it over the back of his chair, rolled up his shirt sleeves, made his way back to the window and gently pulled down the blind. But this time instead of returning to the front of the classroom he crossed the room and stood directly in front of Tony. I shrank in my seat.

Then, in one swift movement, Mr. Currie slapped Tony across the face and said,

Now go ahead and put it back up!

Tony was trembling with rage and I feared for Currie's life. But Tony never rose from his desk and Mr. Currie simply turned, walked away, and continued to teach his lesson as if nothing had happened. Now there was a real man! I have heard it said that teachers and coaches are often some of the most influential people in one's life and that day I was introduced to the man who would become an inspiration to me for a major part of mine.

Mr. Currie was not only a history teacher, but also Balfour's football coach. I loved football and played it in the sandlot with Alex, Bill, Don and a host of others, but I had never participated in organized sports and many of the players on the Balfour team had played hockey, baseball and minor football since they were knee-high to a grasshopper. But after the incident with Tony I was determined to play football for Mr. Currie and I committed myself whole heartedly to the task. I made the junior team in grade ten and the senior team in my final two years. For the first time in my life I had a role model that I could strive to emulate.

About this time my family moved from our old rental accommodation to a new home in the city's southern reaches of Whitmore Park and I found it increasingly difficult to maintain my studies, football practices, and continue my associations with the old gang at the Victory Tea Room. I was also making new friends, developing a new respect for others in a school I had once detested, and football was fast becoming a major dynamic in my life.

Balfour boasted the cities finest football program and my love for the game grew as we celebrated the city, South Saskatchewan and provincial high school football titles and a record setting forty game winning streak. Things were looking up. I had new interests, new friends, a new school, a new home, and a new hero – a mild mannered, soft spoken history teacher named Mr. Currie.

4
Dad's Best Afterthought

1960 was a special year – that was the year my mother brought home my baby sister. I was sixteen when Laurie was born and she quickly became the most spoiled child the world had ever known. I suppose that was only to be expected since being born so long after Diane and I she seemed like an *only child*. Me, I wanted a brother and when my mother first told me she was expecting I jokingly told her not to bring it home if it wasn't a boy. But this little girl soon became the apple of her brother's watchful eye.

Sadly, however, my mother's love for me was often deeply resented by my father, who mistakenly seemed to believe that each of us has only a certain amount of love at our disposal and which could be imparted to others. Subsequently, he interpreted her love for me as somehow being a threat to his own position. Years later she expressed those very thoughts to me in a letter in which she wrote,

I have always believed a mother and son are something special, especially the way I have always felt about you. I have been laughed at many times, and mocked about cutting my apron

strings on you. . . . I never really say how much I love you to anyone, as I have been told before to love my son, but don't be in love with him. Believe me I know the difference.

Perhaps such underlying tensions reside in every family when young men grow nearer to adulthood, and their inherent pack-leader mentalities kick in and the male psyche drives them from the den in search of their individuality. Perhaps such things are normal – perhaps. But one thing I do know, with the arrival of this baby girl, the dynamics of our family began to change. My father seemed less and less threatened, his feelings of jealousy waned and as Laurie Kathleen became the central focus of his life the relationship between us slowly began to evolve into one of relaxed friendship.

It wasn't that Laurie did not furnish both my mother and father with many added nights of worry, heartburn, and frustration, but she struck some inward chord in my father that had never been reached before and in so doing found a method of communicating with him that none of us had ever achieved before. Perhaps they shared some inward kindred spirit that could simply not be denied, but her care for him in the later years of his life and her presence at the bedside of both my mother and father as they passed away from this life proved beyond any shadow of a doubt that she truly was - *the best afterthought dad ever had.*

5
Where to From Here?

What do you do when you graduate high school at seventeen with no intentions of furthering your education? I suppose you just go to work. Fortunately, I received an offer of employment in my last few months of high school. A small country newspaper, a hundred and thirty miles away, called on the recommendation of my art teacher, with the offer of a job as an advertising artist for their weekly paper. I accepted and moved away to the little town of Swift Current to start the next phase of my life.

But somehow living in a rooming house with eight other people is not much of a living, although for the lady who ran the place it was heaven on earth. She had raised twelve children and now found that catering to a mere eight borders was akin to semi-retirement and the money was a whole lot better. She was a kind, motherly soul, I liked her and I loved her cooking. I knew I could grow to like it there, but inwardly my soul was restless.

The job was okay too, creating and selling newspaper ads to local businesses. Now of course, this was long before computers when *typeface* had to be set by hand on something called a *linotype machine.* Along side each machine hung a lead bar that was melted and molded into type face as the operator typed the text onto a keyboard. I still remember the old man with the hunchback and the twisted facial expressions that daily collected the used type, carried it to the back room, and remolded it back into those long lead bars to be used on the linotype machines, over and over again. It wasn't until many years later when the dangers of working in such close confines with *lead* became public knowledge that I realized his condition was more likely caused by lead poisoning than any quirk of Mother Nature.

But I did learn a few lessons in my short lived newspaper career, not the least of which was the night I let a fellow worker and roommate borrow my car – he never came home – and the next morning I walked three miles to work. It only had to happen once. I also discovered what it meant to work hard and to support myself, but the work-a-day world was just not in my seventeen year old blood and after only a few months I was lured back to the big city in hopes of fulfilling my dream of continuing to play football. Sadly, however, that dream soon vanished when I realized that at the next level my new coach was no Mr. Currie.

The coach of the Regina Rams was Bert Ianonne and he was a different from Gord Currie as night was from day. He favored certain players who instantly took advantage of the situation by not showing up regularly for practices and yet still retained the privilege of playing in the games. Of course they always showed up on Friday night before a Saturday game and I still remember one of them when he was told he could be in the starting lineup the next day saying,

But coach, I haven't been here all week, I don't know any of the new plays you put in.

To which Ianonne responded,

Well, don't worry about it we just won't use any of those plays this week.

Meanwhile, those who had practiced hard all week stood by in dismay. Sadly, the scene was constantly repeated and not surprisingly the coach's favorites were continually thrashed on the football field while the true essence of the team stood by helplessly on the sidelines. Finally, in disgust I quit before it could become any more unbearable.

Interestingly, many years later I read of a study conducted amongst football players across the entire nation. One of the questions they were asked was to rate what they considered to be a coach's most important attribute. A wide range of characteristics were presented including everything from *knowledge of the game*, to *intensity*, but the overwhelming number of respondents came back with just one answer – *fairness*. I never doubted for a moment the integrity of that study because I had learned that lesson for myself while watching the opposing styles of coaching practiced by Currie and Ianonne and I had long since vowed that fairness would be uppermost in my mind when I became a football coach.

Life continually presents us with lessons, both positive and negative, from which we may borrow the concepts and ideals that will ultimately formulate our own character. For instance, while it is easier to learn to win and more difficult to learn to lose, there is nothing that says we have to learn to *like losing*. But neither the lessons of winning nor losing exceed the value gained from learning the much greater lesson of just *treating people fairly* whether you win or lose in the process.

So with the end of my football playing aspirations it was back to reality for me and since I had resigned my job at the newspaper it was back to selling shoes, something I had done part-time during my high school years. I earned a whopping $37.50 a week for two years until I was appointed assistant manager at $42.50. Wow!

Thankfully, it was during those frustrating early years that I met the woman who would one day become my wife. Gail attended Scott Collegiate, was the Social Convener of the Student Council and well known to my friend Alex, who incidentally told me she would *never* go out with someone like me. Unknowingly, our paths had already crossed on several occasions, once at my own home when my buddy Alex dropped by with a few friends – Gail amongst them. At that time I was at home with my girlfriend Cheryl, who eventually married Alex and I paid Gail little or no attention.

The second occasion was much more fascinating. After I had graduated, my old football coach, Mr. Currie, asked if I would assist the team by scouting an upcoming opponent – Scott Collegiate. I was absolutely delighted; after all, Scott's team was largely comprised of my old buddies. A friend accompanied me that day to the Scott practice field and we had no sooner arrived and taken up our position across the road when our interest was perked by two gorgeous girls walking by the practice field on their way home from school. In my mind's eye I can still plainly see her, a blonde, wearing a blue sweater, a pleated white skirt, blue knee-high socks and white running shoes. And in catcall-like fashion I impolitely blurted out,

Hey, I like blue socks, no matter what color they are.

Of course, she ignored me.

A short time later, when we began dating, we recalled those occasions and I also discovered that Gail and her friends would not pass by the Victory Tea Room, my old hangout, without crossing to the other side of the street. The riffraff that frequented the place were not the kind of people they cared to acknowledge. Little did she realize then that I had been one of them.

Who can explain how two people from diametrically opposed backgrounds come to meet, fall in love, and spend the rest of their lives together? Maybe the person was right who said,

"Coincidence is God's way of remaining anonymous."

Surely unseen forces are at work behind the scenes in the circumstances and little coincidences of our lives. And even if love doesn't make the world go around, it sure can make the trip worthwhile.

6
Too Young to Die

Sometimes steelworkers, carpenters and electricians walk off the job or go on strike. Even public servants have been known to man the picket lines to prove a point, but *doctors on strike?* Who ever heard of such a thing? And yet it was a doctor's strike, or at least their decision to *work-to-rule,* that lay at the root of my mother's problem. She had a child on her hands with severe stomach pains and no doctor willing to help. In fact, the only advice her doctor offered was to, *put a hot water bottle on it and send him to bed.* His advice almost killed me and even now I can only vaguely recall trying to convince the ambulance driver not to use the siren enroute to the hospital. I didn't want the neighbors to notice. Pride does funny things to people. The diagnosis was a ruptured appendix and the surgeon, Dr. Cardiff, made it very plain that unless they were lucky and surgery performed immediately I would be dead within the hour. My father's anger became almost uncontrollable.

My dad was what one might call a truly *hard case,* raised in England in an area frequented by gangs of marauding Gypsies, he and his school mates literally fought their way to school every single day. During the depression years in Canada he had ridden freight trains across the country in search of a job with the vast hordes of other transients. He spent many nights in hobo camps and some in jails. Even after he married and became a well known singer and radio personality he still fought his way through a vast number of barrooms and dance halls. I still remember seeing him one morning standing before the bathroom mirror with his face scraped and raw by having been rubbed in the gravel. In my eighth year of school, the police, searching for him, followed me to school thinking he might try to contact me. I just laughed. It proved how little they knew about him. For recreation he sometimes took part in bull riding on the rodeo circuit and the cowboys said he was *a man to ride the river with* – it was their ultimate compliment.

But although my dad was anything but the ideal father during those years we always knew that he would protect his family with his last dying breath and so that night in the emergency ward of the Regina General Hospital when he told Dr. Cardiff that if I died the doctor who had provided the misguided misinformation would pay for it with his life, no one who even vaguely knew my father, doubted for a moment that he meant exactly what he said.

Fortunately for Dr. Cardiff, he was not the man who had offered the ill-advised diagnosis – his name was Macintosh, and an apparently more incompetent doctor could not be found in the entire city. But Cardiff clearly understood the situation, and he calmly assured me he was going to do everything he could to help me. By that time the painkillers had taken effect and I was strangely unafraid, although for the first time in my life, I realized that I might *actually die*. Strange how when you're young you think you're somehow immortal and take life so much for granted until one day when it dispenses its own brand of reality.

When I opened my eyes, the nurse at my bedside quickly jumped backward to defend herself and only after she realized I was in my *right mind* did she explain that only yesterday, in a delirious state, I had taken a rather unorthodox swing at her. And then she casually explained that it wasn't really that unusual, that people do strange things when they are in severe pain or

28

recovering from the effects of anesthetic. Still the operation had been four days earlier.

Her name was *Lorraine Hirsch* and surprisingly, she knew me. It seemed she had also attended that little one room school house - Lorne School. She also reminded me that I had actually attended an after-school children's Bible class in her home in grade three. Lorraine was a good nurse and apparently a committed Christian.

Hospitals were very different during the 1950's. Private rooms were unheard of except for the famous or the very wealthy. But for the rest of society a hospital stay could be a real eye-opener. When I finally came to my senses I found myself in a large room with about twenty other men. The beds were arranged like those in a military style barracks. Thankfully, each bed at least had privacy curtains that could be moved along a tracking system to provide visual privacy if nothing else. Sound was another matter – everything said to any nearby patient could be clearly heard by those in adjacent beds.

The blackened toe on the foot of the man in the bed on my immediate left shocked me. The covers had been purposely laid aside to prevent irritation of the darkened area, and although his doctor pulled the curtain to eliminate my view, his conversation with his farmer-patient could be plainly heard.

How did you do this?

Well, I was working in the yard and I dropped a mallet on my foot.

What did you do about it?

Well, nothing really I just cursed a few times and kept right on working.

How long ago did you do this?

Oh, it was about a year and a half ago.

Why didn't you do something sooner?

Well, I just didn't think it was a problem until it started turning black.

Well, it's a problem now, said the doctor, opening the curtain. *We'll just have to hope for the best.*

For several days I watched pieces of that toe fall off. It was a truly disgusting sight. And then one day I awoke to see him being wheeled to the operating room on a gurney. Hours later he returned – they had removed his foot. A week later he lost his leg. They expected he might lose his life, and although I was there three weeks it was not long enough to see the final outcome of his struggle. But I learned a lesson from that farmer about casually letting things lie that I hope I'll never forget.

Still my hospital lessons didn't end with the farmer and every night I listened to the moans and groans of the patients in that extended ward. Sometimes I imagined myself in a field hospital in Holland or France during WWII. The cries of the sick and the dying were everywhere. Sleep was continually interrupted and each morning dawned to see another empty bed or a body with a sheet pulled over its face. They preferred to move the bodies out at night when fewer people could observe the procession but with usually only one nurse per ward that wasn't always possible.

Draining tubes from my stomach and side were helping to remove the poisons from my body, but the pain was often unbearable. I begged for the morphine that had been cut off after the first twenty-four hours and then one day Dr. Cardiff arrived, pulled the curtain surrounding my bed, uncovered my wound and shook his head. It was a clearly a bad omen. A look of concern crossed his face. My swollen incision was clearly infected and then without any hesitation he took out his scalpel, rinsed it with alcohol, and said, *You might want to hold onto the bed.* I reached both arms over my head and grasped the vertical iron rods that formed the white metal headboard. Then he added, *Have courage.* Without anesthetic or hesitation he cut a one inch opening at the top and bottom of my incision. The pain was intense but the smell was worse.

Slowly, I began to mend and my girlfriend Gail's visits were the healing balm I needed. Three weeks later I left the hospital but two days after that I was back in Cardiff's downtown office for another *ad lib* surgery — as he reopened my draining incision, but this time I was clearly on the mend. My mother was right when she said, *Only the good die young.* I knew I wasn't that good and besides — I was too young to die.

7

Bugs and All

My closet contained more than twenty pairs of the latest men's shoes and it was perfectly natural. When you sell shoes for a living, you're always the first to take advantage of those in-store bargains. My two year stopover in the shoe business should easily have been expected since it was my part-time job all through my high school years. My friend Alex had arranged that first *real* job at the Bata Shoe Store and the experience made me a prime candidate for the full-time job at the newly opened Reward Shoe Store in the Golden Mile Plaza.

Working with the public can be a trying experience and I was soon exposed to a whole range of people who looked down upon shoe salesmen as though they had derived from some lower life form. Sadly, it's an attitude I have also seen repeated to waitresses, check-out clerks and others in the service industries, an attitude of superiority that encourages rudeness and sometimes even cruelty.

One personal example of such rudeness is burned into the recesses of my mind like one of those irritating television commercials that can never quite be eradicated. It happened during my shoe store days and at the time I happened to be serving a young girl, perhaps thirteen years of age. Her mother had shown me the model of shoe the girl wished to try on. Yet even then I sensed something caustic in her mother's attitude. I measured the young ladies foot, retrieved the shoe, and slipped it onto her foot and she paced back and forth testing its fit and comfort. Then enthusiastically, she asked her mother if she could wear her new shoes home. Her mother obliged. I packaged her old shoes and completed the sale. And then came my apparent mistake, just as they were leaving the store, by force of habit, I said to the young lady, *Thank you, I hope you'll come in and see us again sometime.* It was apparently the opportunity her mother had been looking for because she turned to me and rudely replied, *That's not likely, she's blind you know!* Her statement cut me to the quick. I felt like saying, *No, I didn't know, but thanks for telling me.*

Throughout the entire service I hadn't the slightest idea that the young lady could not see. In fact, to this day I am amazed that she concealed it so well. But my heart went out to her when I saw that she was as embarrassed at her mother's statement as I was. I suppose that's why the synonyms for rudeness are words like *ill-mannered, ungracious, unpolished,* and *barbaric.* It seemed to me a very sad thing to do to your daughter. This young lady had obviously enjoyed our short interaction. She may even have appreciated the fact that I had not recognized her disability. Perhaps it was one of the few times in her life when she was treated like everyone else. But it was clearly obvious to me that she handled her disability better than her own mother did.

There were only three of us at Reward Shoes, Barry, Keith and me. Barry was the manager, I was the assistant manager. Keith was other full-time employee. It was sort of like government, more managers than workers. There were, of course, a number of part-time employees who came in during busier periods. Now in her heart, Gail has always been a matchmaker and when she introduced her friend Ruth to Keith there was an instant connection and they immediately became an *item.* Unfortunately, about the same time the Reward Shoes hierarchy decided to downsize and since Keith was low man on the totem pole he would have to go. But Keith and Ruth had just announced their pending marriage and Keith simply could not afford to lose his job and since I had already begun my application process to join the Royal Canadian Mounted Police, I volunteered to take the bullet. I left and Reward Shoe Store realized an instant payroll savings of $42.50 a week.

I wasn't unemployed for long however and I soon found a position in a *management trainee* program at a five and dime store named Kresgee's. Kresgee's was the main competitor with the F.W. Woolworth Company. Of course, everyone who has ever taken a *management trainee* position knows it's really just a fancy name for a job where you work extra hours without overtime pay. After all, you're *management*.

Although my intent was still to join the RCMP, I enthusiastically approached my new position. If things worked out, I would forgo joining the police force, maybe even one day become a store manager. So I keenly devoted myself to the company, that is, until I began to learn first hand that something was rotten in the Kresgee Kingdom. Firstly, I learned that if a store caught fire the store manager was automatically fired. No questions were asked, no explanations acceptable, even arson provided no acquittal from the summary conviction of Head Office. The manager was held responsible regardless, of the evidence or the circumstances.

My second disillusionment surfaced when the manager decided to fire the lady who worked in the record department. In the early 1960's there were no cassette tapes, no CD, and certainly no such thing as an IPod. The rock'n'roll era was in full swing and music was produced on vinyl discs which were recorded at 78, 45 or 33 1/3 speeds and our record department sold them all. Not surprisingly, teenagers swarmed the record department every time a new hit single made the charts and Saturdays in the record department were wild and tumultuous affairs but in spite of the confusion that occasionally reigned there, it seemed to me the young lady who ran the department did a fairly decent job. But then who was I to say?

Mr. Scott, the store's assistant manager, was a real *piece of work*. He would often have our junior management team, which consisted of four people, move entire sections of the store from one side of an aisle to another simply because he believed more people looked to the right than to the left when they entered that part of the building. Hours and hours would be spent rearranging shelving and products only to have them reversed a week later when sales figures did not support his initial premise. But the store manager, Mr. Baron, *loved* Mr. Scott. And often it seemed Mr. Scott was making the majority of the in-store decisions. And not surprisingly it was Mr. Scott who decided the lady in the record department should go.

Unfortunately, the Saskatchewan Labor Code, demanded that when someone was fired they were entitled to severance pay. In this case two weeks pay would be required, but the law also stated that any person who simply quit their job was entitled to no such benefit. So to Mr. Scott the answer was rather obvious and his instructions to all of us were, *Just ride her until she quits.* I alone refused. It was the first black mark on my short-lived Kresgee's career. I wasn't surprised that Scott's plan worked to perfection and three miserable weeks later the poor girl quit and left the store in tears. It was a management coup and Mr. Scott never forgot my lack of support in his venture.

My promotion to the Head of the Receiving Department did not meet with Mr. Scott's approval, but the store manager made the decision and he was forced to live with it. So I labored in the bowels of the basement receiving, checking and overseeing the pricing of all the incoming products from cold cream to chocolate bars and for a short time things seemed to move along with little interference from Mr. Scott, although at times he would come down and rummage through yet unpacked cartons, tossing merchandise here and there in search of some hot product he was waiting the arrival of, never stopping to recognize that once he opened a carton without thoroughly checking its contents that we could no longer make any claims if merchandise were missing, of course, those trivialities never troubled Mr. Scott.

Interestingly, my basement domain also included a locked room that contained more valuable items like giftware and jewelry but it also contained the store's considerable assortment of candy and confectionary items, the latter of which were more likely stored there to prevent employees from nibbling away at the profits. The fact that it was locked also testified to management-employee trust level. So the *Candy Room*, as it was called, was filled from floor to ceiling with cases of chocolate bars and twenty-five pound boxes of sweets and nuts to be sold in bulk. It was indeed a confectioner's delight, a place where anyone with a sweet tooth would willingly be condemned to solitary confinement. But it was also to be the location from my next confrontation with the iniquitous Mr. Scott.

One morning the young lady that supervised the candy department came to me and told me she had seen some *bugs* crawling around inside a box of mixed nuts. I asked her to show me the box, retrieved it, and placed it next to the conveyer belt and I assured her it would disposed of when the garbage was collected later that afternoon. At least, that was the plan, until Mr. Scott made his daily inspection forte into the lower bowels of the building. My inquisition began when he spied the condemned box of mixed nuts.

What's this box of nuts doing here?

Oh, the candy girl saw some bugs in it.

Well, why is it here?

I left it there so I could throw it out with the garbage. Then I added, *By the way; I think you might want to check the candy room in case there are any more problems. I know we have a contract with a fumigation company that takes care of problems like that.*

Scott responded, *That would cost too much money,*

Actually, I said, *I believe it's a yearly contract that we pay for. It shouldn't cost us anything.*

I know about the contract! It's not the contract. It's the cost of the candy! If we fumigate that room we'll have to dispose of all the candy!

So what?

Don't be ridiculous. We're not throwing out that much candy.

Well, my job is to tell you. I told you. The rest is up to you.

So what about that box by the conveyer belt?

What about it? I told you, it's there to be thrown out with the garbage.

He checked the labeling and his reply astonished me,

Do you realize that those are some of the most expensive nuts we sell? That's a twenty-five pound box. Roll some paper out on your workbench, spread the nuts out on the paper and pick out the bugs. Then put the nuts back into the box and put it back in the candy room.

He didn't appreciate my rebellious response as I headed out the door,

Pick them out yourself. I'm going for lunch.

It was less than an hour later when I returned that I saw Peter, my assistant and Mr. Scott's number one protégé, laboriously picking his way through the mixed nuts. I could only shake my head and although the thought occurred to me to call the Health Department; I did nothing and simply went back to my other obligations. It was 1962 and those nuts sold for 99 cents a pound – bugs and all.

8
Hurry up and Wait

It didn't take long to realize my retail management career with Kresgee's would be short lived. And since I was still in the throws of applying for the RCMP, I decided to seek some other employment that would tide me over until my application was either accepted or rejected. But an application process I expected to take only months stretched into two and a half years and at times seemed completely hopeless.

Since I have never been a math wizard I wasn't surprised when I failed the mathematics examination of my application. And since I couldn't re-apply for another six months, I purchased some mathematic text books, buckled down and used the time to bone up on my math skills or lack thereof.

At the same time I knew that all *Mounties* also had to be able to swim and I couldn't. In fact, I was afraid of water, a fear I suspect began the day my Uncle Jimmy decided he would teach me to swim by throwing me into a lake. Although I managed to save myself while he stood by laughing uncontrollably on the shore, I quickly recognized the failure of his warped philosophy.

Still, I envied children whose parents put them into swimming lessons, or for that matter, lessons of any kind and I often wished I had been even a little encouraged to learn to swim, skate, or hit a baseball, but those were just not the things our family did. Subsequently, many of my childhood memories are filled with the reminders of being the last one chosen for the pickup baseball game, or making excuses to avoid accompanying friends to the neighborhood swimming pool. Even though some athletic abilities began to emerge during my high school years, even so, I remained far behind my contemporaries in most sport related areas. But the time had come – I had to learn to swim!

With high hopes I joined the YMCA and began to take swimming lessons. I was determined to learn to swim even if I drowned in the process – and I probably would. Taking swimming lessons when you're a little older can be embarrassing, especially when most of the beginner's class is very young. So in every class I pushed myself to do just a little better than my classmates - it proved my undoing.

The YMCA pool was eight feet at the deep end and I soon could splash around just enough to get safely in and out. Then one day we played a game that involved diving to retrieve hockey pucks on the bottom of the pool and since I was not about to let any ten year old collect more pucks than me, I persevered and I won the *hockey puck challenge* and I only assumed that the fuzziness in my head was some kind of reaction to the chlorine or our over-extended lesson time. The next morning told a different story when I awoke to find my pillow soaked in blood.

My broken eardrum would not pass muster and even with my RCMP acceptance letter in hand I was once again rejected – this time on medical grounds. Even the specialist was not overly optimistic. The only remedy was surgery – eight hours of surgery. I was crushed. My hopes of joining the RCMP had been dashed yet again and not only had I not learned to swim; I had seriously hindered any further chance to fulfill my dream. Oddly, it was one of the few times in my life when my dad provided sound advice. He encouraged me to continue. It was one of the things I admired about him – he was no *quitter* and he wasn't about to let me quit either. I agreed to the surgery and decided to hang in for one more chance.

Following months of appointments, during which time drops of an acid solution were applied to my damaged eardrum to prepare it for surgery, I awoke to find my head bandaged and a serious lack of balance. I had never realized before just how much one's equilibrium is controlled by the workings of the inner ear. My arm was sore too, because they had removed a vein from it to repair the damaged eardrum. But the doctor was optimistic that the operation had been successful although it was going take considerable time to heal – it seemed to me just another way of saying *"Hurry up and wait."*

9
Politics of a File Clerk

Government agencies can usually be found operating in one of two states – either they are in a *comatose* condition in which little or nothing is being achieved, or in a state of *crisis*, in which everything should have been done yesterday. In government there is virtually no middle ground.

I first recognized that fact after I left my job at Kresgee's and took a position as a low-level file clerk with the Saskatchewan Government Insurance Agency in Regina. I still needed time to heal from my ear surgery and a steady job to support myself while my application with the RCMP continued. Besides, if the RCMP didn't work out I was going to need a job anyway – preferably something with a future. But filing day in and day out soon becomes tiresome and so together with a couple of other entry level clerks I began to take an interest, if somewhat facetiously, in politics.

Now at this time a socialist party, known as the CCF, was in power in the province of Saskatchewan and had been for more than twenty years, but since as young idealists we believed that being radical was more fun that being mainstream, we assumed the banner of the opposing Liberal Party and thereby anointed ourselves official critics of the government. And there was much to criticize since, as history demonstrates, political parties that rule for long periods of time soon begin to see themselves as ruling more by Divine Right than by the grace of the citizenry that duly elected them. And besides, it is always easier to criticize those in power than to actually govern oneself.

Corruption masquerades in many different forms and even generally honest people can become entangled in its outward tentacles, like cheating on taxes, pilfering office supplies or padding expense accounts. But the synonyms for corruption are still words like fraud, dishonesty, and even bribery. And notwithstanding that someone may be nothing more than a lowly file clerk some forms of dishonest behavior are so blatant that there seems not to have been even the slightest attempt to conceal them. And sadly, such was the case at the Saskatchewan Government Insurance Agency, where even file clerks knew that department managers, whose jobs never took them beyond the confines of their offices, were being granted government vehicles for personal use. Indeed, many ordered not only the make and model of vehicle they desired but even the color they preferred, then subsequently left those vehicles at home for their wives to drive during the day and took local transit to work. So there was no shortage of ammunition for our trio of outspoken Liberal file clerks. Yet our comments were always ignored and our warnings never taken seriously, at least not until the provincial election.

But apparently it wasn't just a few file clerks who recognized the shortcomings of the government and that spring the ruling party was defeated at the polls and CCF house of cards collapsed practically overnight. I will never forget the mood in the offices of the Government Insurance Agency on the morning after that fateful election. Little huddles of people could be seen skulking in managers' offices and in worried conferences around the water coolers. And not surprisingly, no one would acknowledge or even talk to those nasty, traitorous junior file clerks! It was almost as if we had personally sabotaged the ruling dynasty. It was really quite amusing.

But the new Liberal Government moved swiftly to make its impact felt. All government issued vehicles were immediately recalled and all essential government owned vehicles ultimately replaced with a standard make, model and color – dark green and designated by the letter *G* on their license plates so that they could be easily identified by the public who were also encouraged to report any suspected misuse.

It was a sad day for my poor mother who was a staunch CCF supporter with the ignorant attitude of, – *If it was good enough for my father, its good enough for me.* But dad and I were not quite that gullible and we always voted for the man first and only if we could support his party platform. They say *"a new broom sweeps clean"* and it seems that every party that governs too long is in need of serious housekeeping. Sadly, the new Premier failed to promote, or even acknowledge the work of his underground file clerks, but that didn't really matter because I had received another written invitation from the RCMP and was scheduled to begin training in October 1964 – if I could just pass the final medical examination.

10
"*Déjà Vu Doc*"

Life spins for each of us a web that is absolutely unique and completely exclusive. Its web is formed strand by strand when the intersecting of *time, chance* and *circumstances* bring us into contact with other individuals as we journey from birth to death. Just think about this – no other person in this entire world, in all of history or even the unlimited future, will ever cross paths, in *time, chance* and *circumstance* with *exactly the same people* as you do. Life spins each of us a personal web and sometimes the way in which it weaves its pattern borders on the truly bizarre. My final RCMP medical examination was to be no exception.

When the examining doctor saw the scar that ran the length of my stomach and the scar from the draining tube on my side and read the name on my application he turned ghastly pale. I knew, he knew, and he knew that I knew. Yet it was the first time I had seen Dr. Macintosh the man who had misdiagnosed my ruptured appendix years earlier, face to face. Here was the man whose life hung in the balance while Dr. Cardiff performed the surgery that saved my life. Macintosh was English and he was arrogant. But the look on his face betrayed a man clearly shaken and he couldn't wait to get me out the door. But when he looked into my ear he stuttered and sputtered his observation of what he saw and only reconfirmed his own sad incompetence as he said,

You have a perforated eardrum!

That happens to be a repaired eardrum, I replied.

Well, I'll have to refer you to a specialist, I can't approve that. It's a perforated eardrum as far as I'm concerned.

I smiled as I sensed his quandary. I could see he wanted, in the worst way, to give me a passing grade, but now he was caught once again between his own incompetence and his lingering fear of my father. So I relieved his anxiety and I said, *Go ahead and send me to a specialist.* His charlatan face betrayed his obvious relief. He scribbled out the request and handed it to me.

The specialist laughed out loud, signed the papers, and two months later I was sworn into the Royal Canadian Mounted Police to begin training in October 1964. I could hardly have guessed that by the time I was finally accepted I would have followed an application process that lasted two and one half years and included an eight hour ear operation. I was finally on my way — *but I still couldn't swim.*

11

What's an Electroplated Hoof Pick?

In 1964 RCMP training was tough and in some cases *sadistic* and equitation, horseback riding, was at the core of the Force's training system which followed the formations, commands and movements of historic British cavalry units. Each troop consisted of thirty-two men who would learn to perform the routines which can still be seen today in the presentations of the force's famous Musical Ride and on graduation day would perform their version of the famous ride for dignitaries and specially invited guests again confirming the old adage which says, *The outside of a horse is good for the inside of a man.*

But to raw recruits the eighty high-strung horses in the stables at Regina's training center were nothing if not intimidating and the legendary, even myth-like, reputations of their kicking, biting, and explosive natures only stoked the fear and apprehension of that first dreadful ride for every newcomer. And obviously, city boys, like me, who knew nothing about horses, were especially vulnerable.

Fortunately, senior troop members, those who had been in training already for several months, were not only familiar with the horses and their tactics, but were more than willing to help those freshly-anointed recruits with their seemingly sound advice. That was when I first learned about the *electroplated hoof pick*.

The buttons and brass on RCMP uniforms had to be polished daily and could easily consume an hour a day in maintenance time. The brass on horse *tack* (bridles, harnesses and saddles) was no exception. Every night before a ride the recruits would learn from a list on the stable's bulletin board which horse they were assigned to ride, and subsequently, which *tack* they were responsible to clean and polish. An inspection preceded every ride to insure the work had been carried out to the satisfaction of the troop's riding instructor. Failing to meet his stringent requirements resulted in extra duties being assigned beyond normal training hours.

So it was because of this continual maintenance of brass buttons, badges and bridles that recruits began to buy additional sets of uniform buttons that had been exposed to a process called electroplating. *Electroplating* applied a permanent sheen to brass objects and so negated requirement for daily polishing. So it didn't take new recruits long before they each bought at least one set of the rather expensive new buttons and it was also about that time when the senior troop members began to advise us that an *electroplated hoof pick* would also save us valuable time in the stables. I don't know if anyone actually bought an *electroplated hoof pick*, although rumors were ripe that some gullible young lads had indeed purchased them at great expense from the mocking senior troop members. But every recruit looked for an edge, and the naïve, like me, sure thought about it. When it came to horses, I'd need every advantage I could lay my hands on even if it meant buying an electroplated hoof-pick.

12
Ride Cowboy Ride!

Our first *ride* was a premeditated disaster. I'm sure our instructor, Corporal Evans, knew full well what the result would be when he took our troop of thirty-two raw, mounted recruits out into the back forty acres on our first day in the saddle. Now anyone who grew up in the forty's or fifty's watching movies of cowboys and the exploits of the U.S. cavalry knows that a cavalry charge is fashioned when a mounted troop advances toward the enemy, shoulder to shoulder, flank to flank, in one long single-line formation and I must admit we looked mighty impressive as we began to walk shoulder to shoulder across that field. The first order was *Walk-march,* and the troop slowly advanced. The next command was *Trrrrooot,* – the horses began to jog. Then came the command *Caaaanter,* – the horses increased their speed to a fast paced lope, then came the final command *"Charge!"* – and all hell broke loose. Horses and riders headed in every conceivable direction. Some horses took to bucking and throwing riders to the ground. Every horse did that which was right in his own eyes. They knew we were green horns and they took great pleasure in the uncontrolled mayhem. It was two hours before the last riderless horses were rounded up. Isn't life funny? Sometimes you can be scared stiff during something that later becomes one of the most comical scenes you can ever remember and my first cavalry charge was one of the funniest scenes I have ever had the frightful pleasure of witnessing.

Following every two hour ride the horses were groomed, watered and fed. Recruits ate after horses. Six AM would find every recruit in the stables cleaning up after the horses and no recruit could eat breakfast until all eighty stalls were cleaned and every horse fed, watered, and groomed. Sweat rolled off every brow in a race to get the job done in order to have time for our own breakfast. If the job wasn't done properly – we simply didn't eat until lunch time and our own breakfast time would be spent finishing the job properly.

Fortunately, the horses weren't as bad as the myths had led us to believe. Some, of course, would bite or kick without the slightest provocation, but we soon could identify the worst offenders and when assigned to one of them we knew we'd have to be vigilant. Still everyone of us got bitten at least once and probably kicked from time to time. Strangely, those horses were uncanny. They could smell a raw recruit the moment he stepped into their stall. Perhaps it was simply because our clothes hadn't yet picked up the *horse smell* that would soon permeate everything we owned and indeed still be present on some of our clothing more than a year after we completed our training.

But as a new recruit, the instant you walked into a stall, that horse sensed it, and in many cases would first test you by leaning into you, pressing you against the side boards until you could scarcely breathe. If a horse could chuckle I'm sure they did more than once as they put the squeeze on us. No doubt one swift punch in the ribs would have rectified such behavior, but anyone caught striking a horse would suffer serious consequences. In fact, on one occasion, I watched as an instructor actually hit a recruit and knocked him to the ground for striking a horse. Recruits were expendable, horses were not. RCMP riding instructors were tough men, of the those posted in Regina, one had ridden with the Swedish cavalry, another had been a rodeo cowboy, and it was said of another that he had a metal plate surgically implanted in his head after having been kicked by a horse. From the strange look in his eye, I never doubted the story was true. But of all the riding instructors, Sergeant Harry Armstrong was the one who most lived up to his name – he was the strongest horseman I'd ever seen.

In fact one day in the riding school as the troop went through its paces, Sergeant Armstrong was riding one of four stallions the RCMP maintained in Regina. It was an animal I'm thankful I never had to ride – but riding stallions was reserved for the instructors. Anyway, on this particular day, some of the mares we rode were in heat and the stallion Armstrong rode was becoming more and more restless and agitated by the minute. He pranced and snorted and danced around with a wild fire in his eyes and that was when the sergeant began to apply his leg pressure on both sides of that stallion. The more that horse rebelled the harder Armstrong squeezed until after what seemed an hour long battle, that brute of a horse, fell forward onto his knees coughing and sputtering with Sergeant Armstrong still in the saddle and it was only when Armstrong released his pressure that the stallion was able to regain his footing. Armstrong had made his point. The stallion knew who was boss. After having ridden horses now for more than thirty years, I still have not seen anyone who could match the leg strength of Sergeant Harry Armstrong.

Every ride during equitation training was an experience. The use of *curb chains* and *spurs,* which allowed for better control of a horse's strength were forbidden for the first eighty hours of riding and that restriction ensured that the horses held the upper hand. Even brute strength is no match for a horse who knows he can have his own way.

Surely the saying *pride goeth before a fall* is true, and not having been *unhorsed,* so to speak, in the first twelve hours of my riding instruction, I was growing more and more confident in my horsemanship abilities. That's when I drew the tallest horse in the stable. I don't remember his name, but I won't forget what he did to me. It was a winter ride in minus thirty degree weather. I was wearing a heavy buffalo robe coat to protect me against the cold, and he threw me to the ground six times in two hours.

I never did catch onto his trick either, but at will he would suddenly drop one shoulder and I would tumble from that English saddle right over his head just like I was doing a front roll on a gym mat. Fortunately, I quickly learned not to let go of the reins when I was thrown. I didn't want to find myself chasing a horse across the parade square. I had watched a fellow recruit do that just the day before to the catcalls of his corporal hollering, *Don't forget to pick up the mail!*

Regrettably, one of the infuriating rules governing remounting was that you could not use the stirrups. So, a short stature, a tall horse, and a heavy buffalo robe make for a long day when you need to remount six times. It was the only time in my life I found myself sweating in minus thirty degree weather. But that horse dispatched my unfounded pride in two short embarrassing hours.

13
Linda on My Mind

Stable discipline was rather unique and recruits who had failed to perform to the satisfaction of the Riding School Staff were disciplined in a number of creative ways. Some would be sentenced to run laps in the soft dirt of the riding school with a feed bag over their head, while others would be condemned to additional after hour duties of *stable management,* a polite name for shoveling manure.

But perhaps the strangest discipline I witnessed took place one sunny morning just prior to my graduation. The six AM cleanup at the stables had just been completed. All eighty horses had been watered, groomed and fed and any moment the command would be given to form up and march off to our own breakfast. Everywhere recruits were marking time in anticipation of the final order.

I was a senior troop member by this time and well accustomed to the routines but in the stall next to me was a raw recruit busily *pretending* to groom his horse. Since he was dressed in his riding boots and breeches it was obvious that he was going to be riding during the first period of the day. Now, his horse had just made a last minute deposit at the back of the stall and thinking he hadn't noticed I pointed to it and politely suggested that he might want to clean it up before Corporal Jessiman saw it. But he simply curled up his lip, shrugged his shoulders and pointed to his watch.

Now Corporal Jessiman was the scariest of all the riding staff and seldom missed an opportunity to deal with those he considered insubordinate. As for me, well, I couldn't help but smile as I continued to groom my own horse and I watched Jessiman approach from that recruit's blind side. In a flash Jessiman was directly behind the stall, legs astride, hands planted firmly on his hips as he called out softly,

Hey fella?

The recruit turned and ridiculously queried,

Me, corporal?

Yes, you fella,

Then Jessiman pointed to the manure pile and the conversation went like this,

Do you know what that is?

To which he feebly responded,

Yes, corporal

Well, how would you like to put that in your pocket?

No, I wouldn't corporal.

I said PUT IT IN YOUR POCKET!

Now riding breeches don't exactly provide what you might call *easy-access pockets,* but I have to give that young man credit because he did it and those ten or twelve *road apples* made quite a bulge as Corporal Jessiman made my day. I can just imagine how popular that rookie was with his troop mates as he carried his excess baggage throughout his two-hour long ride, but I don't doubt he never again failed to clean up after his horse even if it was closing time.

Equitation training varied from the routines of the famous *Musical Ride* to jumping and even exercising on horseback. The horses loved to jump and every jump was both educational and extremely entertaining. First of all, both stirrups were criss crossed over the front of the saddle, the reins followed suit over your horse's neck — so there was virtually no control of your mount. Then the instructor would sit astride his horse at a ninety degree angle to the jump and as each horse became airborne its rider was required to lean forward, turn his body towards the instructor, tip his hat, and say, *Good morning, Corporal.* The results were hilarious, unless of course, it was your turn. Some riders ended up behind the saddle, others hanging precariously under the horse's neck. Maybe one in twenty actually managed to keep from being unceremoniously thrown into the dirt of the riding school. Any rider getting injured was required to remount and complete the jump before reporting to the Post Hospital. One of my troop mates, with several broken ribs received from being thrown into the end wall of the riding school, did exactly that.

But the horses truly loved jumping. In fact some could hardly contain their excitement even when they saw the jumps being erected. And one such horse, named *Sunfire,* could be relied upon to pull out of position, charge past the line of waiting jumpers, and clear the jump before his rider could react. A rider on Sunfire was insured of four or five times more jumps than any of the other horses.

When a troop progressed to a more senior status games could be played on horseback. One such game required the use of a large canvas ball. It probably measured ten or twelve feet in diameter. Four or six mounted riders were split into two teams and the ball was lowered from the ceiling of the riding school where it was kept suspended with large ropes. The mere sight of that ball being lowered would cause some horses to become agitated, kicking up their heels and bucking so as to almost became unmanageable. The object of the game was quite simple

– push the ball to the other end of the riding school – if the ball touched your opponent's end of arena a goal was scored. Several footmen were then assigned to hustle the ball back to its starting position in the center of the arena and another round would begin. Not surprisingly, some horses were clever enough to use their knees to knock the ball forward and could control it while under remarkable acceleration. In such cases, often opposing horses would instinctively turn and throw their hips into the ball to prevent rivals from scoring and change the balls momentum and direction.

But the game most enjoyed by a group of young men was *fighting on horseback.* In this game the troop was split into two equal halves with sixteen men on each side. Saddles and spurs were removed. All combatants removed their shirts – but half the group also removed their *belts* – which became the distinguishing feature between the two teams – one team wore belts, one team did not.

Once ready both teams lined up facing each other on opposite sides of the riding school in a long flank-to-flank formation. Then the command was given, *"Walk-march,"* and riders moved slowly forward. The spacing of each combatant allowed for the riders to pass by one another as they reached the center of the riding school. When all the riders were abreast and interwoven, sixteen facing one direction, sixteen in the other, the instructor hollered *"Go!"*

There was only one rule in the fighting game. *The last team with a rider on a horse was the winner.* It was a scene of selective mayhem. Horses spun around, riders jumped from one horse to another. In my only experience with the game I quickly found myself and my opponent rolling under the horses in a wrestling grip like one of those scenes I had often witnessed in the myriad of western movies I had watched while growing up. It was both invigorating and terrifying. Somehow I became separated from my opponent only to suddenly see the rear foot of a horse coming down squarely upon my chest. In a sudden reflex I drew both hands under her hoof, vainly trying to support the weight. Now a good horse will never step on you if he can help it, and instinctively that horse somehow manage to shift its weight and jump clear, doing no more damage than striking its knee over my right eye, and opening a cut in the process. I scrambled to remount and saw the Corporal shoot me a quick glance, and for a moment I thought I actually detected a note of concern cross his face. It quickly passed. Save for the loss of a little blood I was fine and thankful that horses can sometimes be smarter than men.

Exercise class on horseback would see a large circle of stationary horses standing steadfast as they put up with a variety of calisthenics performed by their riders. Commands like, *"Right leg over"*, *"Left leg over,"* and *"Quick as the best dismount"* were quickly executed. There were *five* dismounts allowed – none of them utilized the stirrups and three required a back flip movement. After each dismount the rider was required to pass under the horse's belly or between the horse's legs before they could remount – again without the aid of stirrups.

Sometimes more sweat was expended in *mounted* exercise class than in the average gymnasium class, but the hazards of course were much greater. Because, while some horses stood patiently others like *Linda* did not. *Linda* was different – she would allow a rider to perform every exercise movement *except one* – when a rider was turned back-to-front in the saddle – Linda *exploded* and when she blew – no one stayed on board. So during exercise class everyone kept one eye on their own mount, and one eye on the unlucky conscript who had drawn Linda.

The Keough brothers were sons of an RCMP officer in New Brunswick. Dave and Derrick were great guys and Derrick kept a weary eye on Dave the day he drew Linda. And since not every riding session included an exercise period they hoped against hope that Dave might avoid the inevitable confrontation with Linda. Sadly, they were wrong. The Corporal ordered the troop into the formation for the exercise routine and Linda seemed to sense that her opportunity was at hand. Almost immediately the commands began, *"Right leg over,"* – now riders sat sideways in the saddle. *"Left leg over,"* – riders returned to their original position. *"Left leg over,"* again riders now sat sideways in the opposite direction. Then the dreaded combination, *"Left leg over,"* and everyone knew that Dave would now be sitting backwards on Linda. Just as expected Linda flew into a rage!

Dave never made the eight-second horn for his rodeo event, and he landed unconscious in the soft mud of the riding arena. I wondered how he could still breathe facedown in the mud, still no one moved to help. The instructor was unsympathetic and immediately ordered Dave's brother, Derrick, to leave his horse and get mounted on Linda. He would then show his brother how it was done.

Then with Derrick mounted on Linda and Dave still lying face down in the dirt the exercise program resumed and Linda again displayed her talents as she threw Derrick into the mud beside his brother. Amid the curses of the Corporal he helped his brother to his feet and both stumbled to the end of the arena. When that ride ended we returned to our dorm to change from our riding clothes into our work fatigues and within half an hour we were again assembled in ranks in front of the water troughs awaiting instructions on caring for the horses. I stood beside Dave in the formation and it was only then, probably an hour after he had been so unceremoniously tossed into the mud that he came to his senses. He turned to me and asked, *"What are we doing here?"* Apparently, he had no recollection of the ride or his personal introduction to Linda.

Swearing was also common place in the stables and instructors often hyphenated words to insert four letter expletives. For me, swearing was just a part of life, but some recruits took it personally and a French-Canadian troop mate complained to the Commanding Officer about the abusive language used by the riding instructors. For two weeks, not a single swear word was heard in the riding school and the instructors conducted every operation as if it were a church meeting. They even called one another *"brother"* instead of *"corporal"* or *"sergeant."* On some mornings our troop would be held back while five or six other troops were released and we'd arrive back at our dorm to find that they had trashed our dorm running over our beds with their unwashed stable boots.

On one occasion Corporal Jessiman stood inches in front of the complainant and hollered, *Someone in this troop is a suck hole Robichaud, you wouldn't know who that is would you?* And when third Class Constable *Robichaud* was finally pressured to quit we entered the stables that day to a barrage of cursing and the cheers from our fellow troops. It was business as usual except for one thing – *I still had Linda on my mind.*

14
Sink or Swim

Physical training instructors in the swimming pool and the gymnasium were cut from the same cloth as their equestrian counterparts, although perhaps somewhat less sadistic. But neither displayed an overabundance of compassion or sympathy.

Being a non-swimmer in the RCMP was not acceptable. Every member must be able to swim. Obviously, a non-swimmer can't rescue someone who is drowning, so I was clearly prepared to learn, but not quite prepared for the tactics that would be employed. Each non-swimmer was paraded to the very edge of high diving board, asked to declare whether they were a swimmer or non-swimmer (which was a bit of a joke since only the non-swimmers had been marshaled there) and then ordered to take one step forward.

I never saw anything quite like what took place in the RCMP pool that day. One man literally *walked* along the bottom of the pool to the shallow end, blowing bubbles over the entire distance. Another thrashed like a drowning man until handed a bamboo pole by one of the training staff. He climbed that shaft like a flag pole in a school yard only to find that the pool was twelve feet deep and the pole only six feet long. He literally sat there perched on the top of that pole with two or three feet of water still over his head. If someone hadn't finally pulled him out, he surely would have drowned. It was morbidly comical.

As for me, I wasn't afraid to step off the board for fear of drowning. I knew I could dog paddle my way to the shallow end; it was my ear that worried me. I didn't know if the graft on my eardrum would hold and the specialist had strongly advised against any testing prior to my enlistment. I closed my eyes, prayed, and stepped off the board. The ear held, and I knew I was going to learn to swim – even if it killed me.

Gymnastics, judo, police holds and boxing were standard fare in the gymnasium, although sometimes an instructor would take pleasure in having a class simply run back and forth in drill formation with a *knee-high* stepping action for an entire sixty minute session while he enthusiastically berated those who became physically sick or couldn't continue.

Boxing was often done with both combatants blindfolded and the remaining members of the troop locking arms to form a makeshift ring. The locked arms highly restricted individual movement and subsequently the worst punches were often received by those forming the ring rather than the boxers. Any recognition of close friendship between troop mates was rewarded with the opportunity to fight one another and no mercy was given to those who were outsized, outweighed or out boxed. Of course all of that might seem unfair, but life by its very nature is unfair, and in reality, policemen don't have the liberty of choosing their preferred combatants.

Even today I can still recall the sick smile that crossed Sgt. Perry's face the day I walked into his gym class with a third degree sunburn. It was Monday morning. I had had Sunday off, had fallen asleep on the beach, and I was as red as a lobster. He stood directly in front of me and with his twisted smile two inches in front of my face he quietly asked,

What do you think we're going to do today, Dolman?

I replied,

I don't know Sergeant.

Then his smile widened and he said,

We're going to wrestle, and guess who's going to wrestle, Dolman?

I didn't have to guess – I knew. And then for the full *one-hour* class I wrestled every members of the troop, one by one – all thirty-one of them. After forty-five minutes I could barely stand. My opponents, knowing my condition but also fully aware that they were not allowed to take pity on me, whispered apologizes when we came to close quarters. By the end of the period I was in sad shape. I had no doubt I should have been hospitalized, but the next period was swimming and for once I was really looking forward to getting into the water.

Unfortunately, I hit the water with a belly flop that almost caused me to lose consciousness. And then as I climbed out of the pool I saw my swimming instructor staring wide-eyed in disbelief. I didn't understand why, until I looked down. The skin on my chest had formed one massive blister from my neck to my waist. He squinted his eyes, tilted his head and asked,

Are you okay?

It was clearly an unorthodoxed response from an instructor. Defiantly, I crossed my arms at my waist, pressed them to my body and drew them up to my shoulders forcing the water from beneath the skin and replied,

I'll manage.

I wasn't going to let them beat me. It had taken me two and half years and an ear operation to get here and they would never get me to quit.

15
Perilous Posting

A few days before final graduation from police training in Regina officers were issued with their badges and given their postings. Since members were employed in every province of Canada anticipation ran wild amongst the recruits as to exactly where they would be ordered to serve. At that time the policy of the RCMP was not to place officers in their home province, supposedly, to minimize the risk of their having to deal with friends or family in the performance of their duties.

Our troop was now down to thirty having lost two of our number during the training period and seventeen were posted to British Columbia. My posting was Kamloops, B.C. and my troop mates were quick to express their condolences. Kamloops was considered a highly dangerous area and in just the last two years four officers had been killed in that region.

One of the officers was Constable Neil Bruce. He had responded to a call that a young girl had been taken against her will in an isolated cabin near Kelowna, B.C. Alone, recognizing the cabin could only be approached by crossing an open field and wanting to appear non-aggressive, Cst. Bruce removed his gun belt, began communicating with the suspect and slowly crossed the field. He was shot dead before he reached the cabin. His assailant was located nine days later near Peachland, B.C. and rather than surrender to police – shot himself. Bruce died April 14, 1965 just six weeks before my arrival in Kamloops.

Three other officers had also been killed in Kamloops on June 18th 1962. They were Constables, Keck, Pedersen and Weisgerber. The incident relating to their deaths began when a game warden crossing a small bridge, that lead to a Department of Highways shed in an isolated area in the city of Kamloops, was approached by a man with a rifle. As the story was related to me the man pointed the rifle at the warden and said, *You're not worth killing.* Obviously, the warden agreed. The man then began to ascend a hill which bordered the southern approach to the bridge. The warden drove away and immediately reported the incident to the police.

Only two of the three officers who responded were on duty at the time the call came in, the third off-duty and unarmed, simply went along for the ride. When they arrived at the bridge and got out of the police car the suspect, who was now in a comfortable position on the hill side, opened fire with a .303 rifle. George Booth was a deadly marksman. Two of the officers died on the bridge. The third made it under the bridge – he was member who was unarmed. Booth simply walked down the hill, shot him, and escaped into the surrounding hills. A manhunt ensued and Booth was subsequently killed by Constable John White.

But George Booth was not forgotten. His father, John, told investigators that before he died he would kill more officers than his son had. One day I would find out personally just how serious John Booth really was. But it was because of these incidents that my fellow troop mates wished me well and were thankful that it was me and Don Pearson headed into the interior and not them.

But on graduation day there was no time for morbid thoughts or needless worries. It was an *all day* affair and a celebration to be remembered for a lifetime. Family, friends and special guests were invited and spent the entire day being entertained by the graduating officers with performances in the gymnasium, swimming pool, and drill hall. Lunch in the Division Mess Hall was followed in the afternoon by the crowning event of the day – the riding display in which the troop performed the maneuvers of the RCMP's famed Musical Ride. Following which the graduates had an opportunity to pose for photographs with their horses for family and friends. It was one of the proudest moments of my life. It had taken nine months of arduous training but I had done it. I was a police officer in one of the finest police forces in the world.

16
First Days are Always the Worst

All of us who were posted to British Columbia headed West in a caravan of vehicles in June 1965. There were seventeen of us in all. Most mates were headed for the coast where posting to the province's largest detachment in the city of Burnaby was akin to being posted to a city police force. But Burnaby wasn't the only large detachment on the West coast and custom seemed to dictate that those first posted to this highly populated area would never be able to leave it.

At Kamloops two of us left the convoy, Don Pearson and me. We were saddened to say goodbye to those we had become brothers with during the hardships of our training, but we were equally excited to be that much closer to actually being police officers. We arrived at Kamloops early in the morning and the Staff Sergeant in charge of the Sub-Division told us to immediately turn out in our full dress red serge uniforms for our presentation to the Commanding Officer. By nine AM we were dressed and waiting for Superintendent Dyck's invitation. The day dragged on. The temperature in Kamloops became scorching hot. The building was not air-conditioned and we stood by becoming more and more uncomfortable by the minute.

Don Pearson was a different kind of a guy. Even in uniform he always appeared to be a little disheveled. Someone said he even looked that way in the shower. Now we had been asked to wait in the single men's quarters which were part of the Sub-Division building and after several hours of being bored to death Don decided to take a look around. Then he found something that fascinated him – a pair of handcuffs. Handcuffs were not issued to graduates and were only to be provided immediately prior to active service. Don was fascinated and without a second thought closed one around his right wrist. It was a tragic mistake - there was no key! My uncompassionate remarks didn't help as I began to elaborate on the scenarios of us being presented to Commanding Officer and him having to salute with a handcuff firmly attached to his right hand. Fortunately, for Don Superintendent Dyck was still in no hurry to receive us and a hasty call for a member to return from patrol supplied the escape mechanism. Lesson learned.

After standing around all day in dress uniform in the heat Dyck finally agreed to see us about four thirty in the afternoon. We stood before him and saluted. He looked at us as if we were aliens for planet Schwartz. His first words were a question,

Which one of you is the best driver?

Don was quick to respond,

He is sir!

Dyck pointed at me

You go to Revelstoke.

He pointed at Don

You go to Hundred Mile House.

Then Don asked,

Tomorrow, sir?

Now!

he grumbled and motioned with his hand for us to get out.

I didn't exactly thank Don for his intervention on my behalf, being a boy from the prairies and unaccustomed to mountain terrain I wasn't the least bit grateful for a posting smack in the middle of the tallest mountains in all of Canada – not to mention some of the countries most dangerous roads. But we parted friends and continued to laugh about Don's handcuff episode. We changed clothes, shook hands, loaded up our cars and headed in opposite directions. Don told me Revelstoke was one of the busiest detachments in the province and he was sure I'd see a lot more action in the coming months than he would in the ranching and cattle country north of Kamloops. He could not have been more wrong. On the 8th of July, 1965, just weeks after our arrival a Canadian Pacific Airlines DC6B exploded over a place called Dog Creek, near Hundred Mile House, B.C. Fifty-two people lost their lives and Don was initiated to the horrifying realities of police work very quickly when he was assigned to collect body parts from the accident scene.

I arrived in Revelstoke at about 7:00PM, and immediately asked directions to the RCMP detachment. I was told it was in the basement of the courthouse building, but I was totally unprepared for what I was about to find. It was one of those old stone structures built by provincial governments in a bygone era, impressive enough from the outside, but inside even its unevenly worn marble floors betrayed its age. Apparently, the detachment portion of the building had been condemned as unfit for use by the earlier B.C. Provincial Police Force. And since I knew they had disbanded the B.C. Provincial Police in 1950 and absorbed their members into the RCMP, this facility was more than past its prime.

I walked up to the half-door, one room office, a lady approached and asked if she could help me, and embarrassingly I said,

I'm looking for the RCMP detachment.

She replied, with a sly smile,

You're looking at it.

There was a twinkle in her eye and an aurora of joy that surrounded her. Later I learned her nickname was *Hap*, because she was always happy and jovial no matter what the circumstance. Her real name was Gladys Dunn and she was indeed one of the happiest people I had ever met.

When Mrs. Dunn introduced me to Sergeant Smith I knew immediately I was meeting the man in charge. Ted Smith was a big man, not only in stature, but also in the eyes of his men who loved him. The kind of boss everyone longs to work for. When I shook his hand I counted myself lucky to under his command.

Sergeant Smith introduced me to Cpl. Vern Myers – one of the biggest men I had ever met. Vern was 6'5" and probably weighed in around 250 lbs. He smiled as he almost crushed my hand and I suspected I was meeting a man with fun-filled larceny running through his veins. Later incidents would confirm my suspicions. It was then Smith told me that I would begin that night at midnight and Cpl. Myers would see that I got off to a good start. Meanwhile I was to check into a local hotel, change into my uniform and report back so that I could have a few hours with Myers before my shift would begin at midnight. Little did I realize at the time that he meant I would work that midnight shift alone.

My room at the McGregor Motor Inn was more than I had been accustomed to, but I also realized I would quickly have to find myself a place to live since the RCMP would only pay for three nights in the motel. Tomorrow I would begin my search. When I had eaten and changed into my uniform I called the detachment and Cpl. Myers came by to pick me up. He began my indoctrination by driving around town. Revelstoke boasted a population of about 5,000 people – or at least that was what I originally thought, but two major construction projects were underway in the area.

Under the terms of a treaty fashion between 1961 and 1964 with the United States, British Columbia agreed to build several dams along the Columbia River. Controlling the water flow of the Columbia, North America's third largest river, would not only reduce destruction from flooding in the United States, but would also provide valuable electrical power, to the profit of both countries. The project was massive and more than 2,300 people would lose their homes to the changes in rising water levels of the basins formed by the four damns.

Mica Dam, the largest to be built would be located at Mica Creek, 148 kilometres north of Revelstoke. When completed it would rise 240 metres in height and 800 metres wide, crossing the narrow valley which bordered Mica Creek. When it was completed it would contain more than 14.8 trillion cubic metres of water in its reservoir. As I arrived in Revelstoke the construction of the Mica Dam was in full swing and two thousand men laboured at the site.

Now if the construction of Mica Dam was not enough to cause policing problems in Revelstoke, the entire roadway – all 148 Kilometres of it was also under construction and work crews were employed at various stations along its length. As Corporal Myers continued I began to get the picture. Strict controls of the road crews and the threat of immediate dismissal for anyone found drinking alcohol at the Mica Dam site meant that the weekend population of Revelstoke swelled to unmanageable numbers. Close to three thousand men would descend upon the city for a weekend of drinking, fighting and general hell-raising.

On Friday and Saturday nights a three block area in the downtown core became no man's land, even for police officers. Patrol cars were regularly bombarded with beer bottles thrown from hotel windows. Everyone arrested could be guaranteed to fight and while the two or three officers on duty were busy removing the worst offenders the reckless abandon would continue unthreatened and unabated. It was perilously close to a complete breakdown in civil order and a police officer's worst nightmare. The small detachment of eight police officers attempting to provide policing for the town, its tributary highways, and a rural area of fifty square miles was simply no match.

Corporal Meyer briefed me as quickly as he could and since it was a week night and the crews were not in town he would leave me on my own to until eight AM the next morning.

If I had trouble I was not to hesitate to call him at home. It was one A.M. when I dropped him off at his home and I was alone.

Harry Galicano, a retired CPR employee and a civilian jail guard was on duty in the office, he was there to answer the telephone and man the dispatch radio. Wow! This was really it. A sense of pride swelled up inside until I came to the sudden realization that this entire town was now relying on me for its protection, and I began to wonder what I had gotten myself into.

It was less than an hour after dropping Vern off that the first call came in. The radio crackled and Galicano informed me that a Supervisor at the Canadian Pacific Railway had telephoned to say that they had an unwelcome visitor in Yard shack who refused to leave. Fortunately, as he spoke, the train station came into view and soon I found myself directed to a small building a short distance down the tracks.

Several men were inside and every one of them looked as though he belonged there. Yet as I entered, a look of relief crossed several faces and the uneasy workers quickly drew my attention to a man sitting in an office chair with his feet up on the desk. Apparently, he wasn't an employee at all, and had just walked in and made himself comfortable. I walked over and asked him to accompany me outside. He rose and moved towards the door. I could sense every eye in the place fixed upon us.

It probably was fairly obvious to everyone there, including this intruder, that I was as green as they come, and it was probably that fact that led to his next action, because no sooner had he started to exit the door, than he suddenly turned back inside, pushed against me, and said, *"I'm not going anywhere!"* That's when I hit him! He fell backwards out the door and I was on him in a minute dragging him to the police car. Then I made my first of two mistakes. I sat him in the passenger's seat next to me, not in the back seat – mistake number one. He quickly rolled down the window and threw a whiskey bottle out onto the road – mistake number two – I had failed to search him.

But that's when the humour of the situation kicked in. Here was a rookie police officer, on his first shift, in a city with only a smattering of street signs – who couldn't find the police station! I must have driven for twenty minutes up and down every street in town trying desperately to find it and too embarrassed to radio Harry for directions. By the time I found the police station my poor prisoner could only shake his head and I couldn't blame him.

I didn't have a clue what the charge was going to be — surely he must have violated some law — well, I'd lock him up and speak to the Corporal about it the next morning. Meanwhile, I had property checks and patrols to make. I had made my first arrest but I sure wasn't very proud of myself. Things couldn't get any worse — or could they?

At 4:00A.M. a call came in from an area across the river known as the Big Eddy — a series of rough and rugged shacks that comprised a local Indian Reserve. The Corporal had mentioned it — he said I was not to go there alone — but pride got in the way. I couldn't bring myself to call for help just a few hours into my first shift.

Our guard, Harry Galicano was smarter than me. He urged me to call for help, but when I refused, he wisely offered me some very sound advice when he said,

Whatever you do don't walk in front of the headlights of your own car.

They were words of wisdom. I shone the lights on the cabin, stepped out into the darkness and soon found myself warmly invited into the shack to settle a dispute between two drunken men. They had been embroiled in an argument when one of them upset the wooden box that served as their table spilling two plates of beans on the floor and the discussion threatened to turn violent. I wouldn't realize just how violent until the next night. But I was able to temporarily diffuse the situation and quickly returned to my other duties.

I don't suppose anyone was more delighted to see the sunrise that day than me. I had completed my first midnight shift and could hardly have known it would be the first of thirty consecutive midnight shifts, without so much as a single day off that I would experience before I saw my first day shift. In fact a roar of laughter greeted me that day when I walked into the office at 8:00 A.M. — with my flashlight in my hand.

By the way, just to finish the story of the Big Eddy incident. The very next night while patrolling in the downtown area I saw one of the men from that incident getting into his vehicle in a downtown parking lot. Naively I drove up behind his car, stepped out, and asked what he was up to. I was simply trying to start a conversation, but he looked at me with a shocked expression on his face. He cocked his head to one side and asked,

How did you know what I was going to do?

Without thinking I responded, *Just smart I guess.*

Then he shook his head and said,

You sure are, I don't know how you knew I was going over to kill that son of a.... I guess you better take me in before I do something stupid.

With that he reached in the back seat of his vehicle, pulled out a loaded rifle, handed it to me and climbed into the back seat of the police car. Since I really had nothing to hold him on I let him sleep in the jail that night and gave him back his rifle in the morning. He thanked me and went home. I guess that was the kind of justice old timers in the R.C.M.P. would have understood.

I won't ever forget those first few shifts – green, unsure, afraid and policing in a volatile town. I could only hope that *first days were the worst* and things would get better.

17
The Roger's Pass

Revelstoke, British Columbia is nestled in the Selkirk and Monashee Mountain ranges. Travellers heading East immediately begin to negotiate the Roger's Pass as they enter Glacier National Park, named after the more than four hundred glaciers that dot its vast landscape. Ten mountain peaks ranging from 8,530 to 11,120 feet provide summer tourists with an unmatched beauty that is traversed by the swirling turquoise waters of the Illecillewaet River which is formed from its namesake glacier located at the summit of the pass.

The Roger's pass was discovered by Major A.B. Rogers in 1881 as a route for the Canadian Pacific Railway. Well known railroad builder William Cornelius Van Horne joined the enterprise in 1882 as General Manager of the C.P.R. He decided that Roger's Pass was the most direct route and proceeded to build it, but construction crews were often terrified by the conditions and the nature of the work involved. Snow fall levels of sixty feet annually at the summit continuously threatened to unleash deadly snow slides upon the rail line and its workers. Conditions were anything but idea. It was a rugged and unforgiving country. One historian wrote,

Construction of a railway to and across Rogers Pass was a formidable undertaking. Roaring mountain streams had carved deep notches into the side of the Beaver Valley. These streams had to be spanned by major bridges at Mountain, Surprise, Stoney and Cascade creeks. These high bridges became favourites with photographers of the day. At Mountain Creek, Ross's forces built a trestle which stretched across a gap in the valley wall for 331 metres and stood 50 metres above the mountain torrent. A few kilometres farther up the line at Stoney Creek, a bridge was constructed, which towered 64 metres above its footings. This bridge was heralded by the engineers of the day as the highest such structure in the world.

Forest fires plagued work crews as they marched up the slopes of the Beaver Valley. Then, later in the year, the weather became excessively wet, changing mud to quagmire and creeks to torrents that ate away at the newly-placed bridge foundations. Ross's efforts to speed the work became bogged down and several times he despaired.

To compound his problems a new and unfamiliar force struck the work crews. Each year, a prodigious quantity of snow falls on the Selkirks. In many places this load rests uneasily on the steep inclines and at intervals becomes unstable and careens down the mountain walls in sudden avalanches. An avalanche or snow slide is an awesome natural force able to snap trees like match sticks as it speeds down slopes at velocities up to 325 kilometres an hour.

The Indians had respected these snow spirits of the Selkirks and stayed clear. James Ross and his men challenged the elements...and the "white death" struck his camps! "The men are frightened," wrote Ross on February 19, 1885 to Van Horne. "I find the snow slides on the Selkirks are much more serious than I anticipated, and I think are quite beyond your ideas of their magnitude and danger to the line." Already seven men had been buried in slides and two killed.

Ross gained the summit of Rogers Pass on August 17, 1885 after six months of trial by avalanche, forest fire and rainstorm. But his problems were not over, there still remained the troublesome descent of the west side of the pass to the Columbia River. [2]

The highway battle began in 1956 and the Roger's Pass highway was opened in 1962, just two years prior to my arrival in Revelstoke. The highway completion was a major undertaking with the threat of avalanches still the major concern. Several snow sheds were built at problem locations but with more than eighty slide paths capable of reaching the highway snow sheds could simply not be built to protect every potential danger spot.

To lessen the danger the federal government hired experts in avalanche control to monitor changing weather conditions and assess the public risk. A dozen or more concrete gun platforms were built at danger spots along the route and a Canadian Army artillery unit was posted at the summit during winter months. The units 105mm howitzer would be used to manually encourage potentially dangerous slides to release under controlled conditions, thereby avoiding any unexpected loss of life. I would learn later, in a very personal way, the seriousness and the tragedy that could surround that operation when four soldiers were killed in an avalanche that was thought to be just another mundane operation.

The Roger's Pass was a beautiful piece of highway on a warm summer's day with its higher altitude resulting in temperatures ten to fifteen degrees cooler than in the lower valleys to the West and on hot summer days highway patrol members would often bargain with one another for the privilege of patrolling East rather than west. No place was prettier in the summer nor uglier in the winter than the Roger's Pass and before my time in Revelstoke was ended I would learn first hand just how deadly it could be.

---

2 http://cdnrail.railfan.net/RogersPass/RogersPasstext.htm

18
Road Hazards

In the 1960's the highway patrol from Revelstoke Detachment was responsible for the Trans-Canada Highway from Sicamous to Glacier, B.C., from Revelstoke north to Mica Creek and south to the Arrowhead lakes. In all about two hundred miles of highway were included.

Corporal Fred Zaharia was in charge of highway patrol and since he held that responsibility alone, I was transferred to highway patrol unit to assist him. Two hundred miles of road – twenty four hours a day – two men – me and Corporal Zaharia, and since he was the senior officer, I was assigned to permanent afternoon shift and the responsibility of being *on-call* between 1:00 A.M. and 8:00 A.M. in case of emergency. In such a vast area emergencies could be expected almost nightly.

Highway patrol duties immediately opened my eyes to the perils that existed on mountain roads. Winter's avalanche threat was replaced in summer by periodic rock or mud slides and the constant danger of forest fires on the heavily treed Monashee Mountains. Heavy rains would also bring flash floods that turned meandering creeks into boiling torrents of water often sweeping large portions of highway into their adjacent canyons. Add to this mix a heavy influx of tourists during the summer months, regular truck traffic along Canada's only major highway together with the careless habits of many drivers, and a recipe for constant disaster was always brewing.

Then, as if all of that weren't enough, the RCMP added to the mix a police officer, born and raised on the flat, bald prairies, who was not all that fond of heights, and the scene of me cautiously making my way to my first accident along a twisting section of highway, siren blaring, dome light flashing, with a bemused convoy of tourists lined up behind wondering if they should actually pull out and pass, and you can probably appreciate the humour of that first encounter. Needless to say, I would soon learn to drive those roads at break-neck speed, even on one occasion in a high speed chase for more than ninety miles from Revelstoke to Golden, B.C. with speeds nearing one hundred miles an hour in pursuit of a stolen car.

When Constable Barry Kingdom joined our unit my work load was reduced to about fifty hours a week, furthermore I was only on call every second week. But since late night calls could be extremely dangerous for just one man, Barry and I had a special agreement. If one of us was on call and needed help the other would willingly go along to assist, but the on-call member would be required to handle the investigation. It was an arrangement that worked extremely well, but it was that arrangement that provoked my first hazardous assault by Mother Nature.

It was winter. It was snowing heavily, and the cloud ceiling was little more than ten or fifteen feet above the highway. The driver of a tractor trailer unit had been negotiating the pass at night in the area of Silver Creek, about twenty-seven miles East of Revelstoke. Due to poor visibility he had rolled his driver's side window down, leaned his head out and tried to make sense of his directions. Caught suddenly unawares by the sharp curves at Silver Creek he suddenly swerved his unit and lost control. The truck flipped on its side, skidded down the highway and came to a rest in a jack-knifed position blocking most of the highway.

Barry was on call and I was only too willing to be his helper. By the time we arrived the driver had been taken to the hospital in Revelstoke by a passing motorist and the danger presented by the overturned rig became apparent. Silver Creek is a series of curves, bounded on one side by a rock wall several hundred feet high, and on the other by a deep drop of a hundred or more hundred feet straight down into the raging Illecillewaet River. Had the truck slid any further it would have plunged into the gorge and the driver may never have been found.

But while the truck blocked most of the roadway, a narrow opening would provide passage past the wreck. The problem was that since the wreck was located between two sharp curves oncoming traffic, as rare as it would be at this time of night, would have to be warned.

Now at this time the town of Revelstoke did not have a tow truck big enough to handle a semi-trailer truck and so Gib Haines, a local resident, was requested at such times, to attach a boom to his logging truck in order to facilitate such an operation. The problem was that this procedure usually took two to three hours and the scene would have to be protected during that time. Furthermore, no radio contact could be made with Revelstoke from this area, and so one of us would have to drive back until radio contact could be made. I volunteered to stay at the scene and Barry headed towards Revelstoke. Seeing him drive away left me with a strangely empty feeling. I was alone in the middle of the Monashee Mountains in the dead of winter.

The heavy snow had already covered the road rash caused by the accident and a foot or more was now blanketing the truck itself. I had known nights in the pass where more than four or five feet of snow could fall overnight and on one occasion needed to stop at a Ranger's station to ask him to take me to a vehicle he had reported as having been involved in an accident. It had snowed so heavily that snow had buried it and only the faint glow of the tail lights could be seen beneath the white mantle.

This was one of those heavy snow fall nights – by the time Gib Haines got here a foot or more of snow would probably be added to what had already accumulated. I secured the scene by placing warning signs and flares on the approaching curves and then paced back and forth waiting for Barry to return. Time dragged. The silence was deafening.

It began with just a muffled sound, the kind of low rumble that causes you to cock your head and listen more intently – to ask yourself if you really heard something or if your mind was just playing tricks on you. But it was definitely there and it was growing louder. That's when the ground beneath my feet began to tremble and I recognized the early warning signs of an avalanche. I knew they often began five or more miles up the mountain side, but at their great speeds could cover that ground in a matter of minutes. Strong winds always preceded them. In fact I had heard of the winds that toppled some ninety train cars loaded with grain near Glacier, just twenty miles away. The scary thing was that the slide following those winds never even reached the rail line. I also realized that I was standing at that moment in the middle of a slide path.

I began to notice snow sifting off the rocks on cliff side of the highway and I searched the low cloud in vain with my flashlight trying to probe its darkness. The noise grew louder and louder. I knew I was in imminent danger. I tried to think of the closest area that might be outside the slide path and I began to run for it as fast as I could. The ground was shaking so hard I could barely keep my balance, until finally, frightened and out of breath I threw myself up against the sheer rock cliff and prayed. (My troubled mind asked if moments like this is why they said there were no atheists in foxholes.)

Snow sifted from the rocks over my hat and down the front of my parka, covering my body with a dusting of powered snow. Then the rumbling began to wane, the shaking subsided and stopped. It was replaced by a deathly quiet. I was alive, but had never felt more alone. I was certain now that the slide had taken the truck into the valley below. Slowly I made my way back – but – the truck was still there. The slide must have come down on the other side of the truck. Then I surmised that Barry would not get back, that the slide would have cut off his approach. Just then my heart swelled at the sight of the police car rounding the corner. I could hardly believe my eyes. I ran to the car and excitedly asked Barry if he had seen a snow slide. He said he hadn't. I hopped into the car and asked him to make his way past the truck and around the next corner.

There it was – a snow slide burying the highway to a height of fifty or sixty feet. It had crossed the road, plunged into the valley below, crossed the fast flowing Illecillewaet River and ascended the opposite mountain to a height of a hundred feet or more. In my disorientation and misinterpretation of the facts – I had been running *straight towards it*! What had kept me from rounding that last curve? What caused me to suddenly flatten against that rock wall? Was it instinct or just dumb luck? As those questions soared through my mind little did I realize just how many more times I would be asking *"what if?"*

Those nasty *'what ifs'* returned again one year on a spotless morning in early March when Cst. Len Grinnell accompanied me to the summit of the Roger's Pass to relay a prisoner from Golden to Revelstoke. Although the countryside was still steeped in snow the road was clear and dry except for an early spring runoff that dampened the roadway inside each of the snow sheds that led to the summit. By all accounts it should have been just a beautiful day for an uneventful drive.

We accepted the prisoner from the Golden Highway patrol members near the Northlander Motor Hotel at the summit of the Roger's Pass and immediately began our descent back towards Revelstoke. I slowed the cruiser as we ascended a grade behind a slow moving semi-trailer truck. He was pulling a double trailer and thankfully his speed was curtailed by his load and the steepness of the incline. Having slowed to about forty or fifty miles an hour, I pulled out and passed him, then entered the long curved snow shed.

Suddenly the patrol car began to slide sideways. The road surface, which had been merely wet just an hour earlier, was now a frozen sheet of black ice. I tried in vain to counter the skid but the vehicle had a mind of its own and with a slight bump it ticked the concrete wall on the opposite side of the highway. It is funny how things slow down at moments like that but – since in those days there were copious reports to file about police car accidents - I heaved a premature sigh of relief as I jumped to the conclusion that we had been spared all but the slightest damage – I thought, *Oh, that's not bad, I can get that fixed myself.* But the inertia created by that minor motion swung the vehicle around causing the rear end to strike heavily against the wall, severely damaging the back of the cruiser, and catapulting us head-on into the opposite concrete wall. Now badly damaged and sitting broadside in the middle of the snowshed we became an instant target for the approaching semi-trailer truck we had just passed. Then, as I turned on the red flashing dome light to warn the oncoming trucker, I heard the prisoner in the back seat screaming,

"We're going to die, we're going to die!"

In a move of self-preservation I jumped from the vehicle, but the concrete tomb in which we were trapped offered no means of escape in either direction. That's when I looked over the roof of the car and saw the cause of our prisoner's anxiety. The semi-trailer truck we had passed had now entered the snowshed and it too was losing control on the black ice. It seemed I was witnessing the action scene from some Hollywood movie. The driver was trying to ride his truck along the left side of the snow shed and it showered sparks over the entire tunnel as he scrapped the tractor and first trailer along the concrete wall. But what terrified me most was his second trailer which was fish-tailing from one side of the shed to the other – completely out of control. I jumped back into the driver's seat resigned to my fate. The trailer loomed to the right of the patrol car, swerved back to strike the wall of the snow and then swung past on the left side, inexplicably missing our vehicle. It was surely a miracle of outstanding proportion. I managed to start the car and somehow drive it out of the snow shed. It's strange how calm you can remain during an incident only to have the shock of it sink in later. Then as we exited the police car a motorist approached and told us that he had just done the same thing moments before us and had been trying to make his way back through the shed to warn oncoming vehicles when he saw us enter and lose control. He had barely escaped with his life.

Now, my partner Len who was so calm I thought he had perhaps been asleep during the whole episode, suggested we make an effort to place warning signs at the opposite entrance of the snow shed. Gingerly, we made our way back through the shed, placed signs at the other end, and were about half way back, edging along the inner concrete wall, when we heard an ominous sound. It was the sound of a vehicle changing gears and accelerating at a high rate of speed. Then, as we looked back, we saw a car enter the shed and lose control ricocheting and bouncing off one wall and then the other like a marble in some surreal pinball game. Fortunately, this highflying acrobat was disabled before it could reach our position. Needless to say, that night I spent another restless night rehashing the *"what ifs"* of another event-filled day on Revelstoke Highway Patrol.

The thirty miles of highway to the south was interrupted by two ferry crossings of the Columbia River. Twice I had spent Christmas Eve and Christmas Day working to recover vehicles and their occupants from the icy waters of the Columbia. In both cases the drivers failed to realize they were driving onto a ferry and each simply snapped the retaining chain at the far end of the barge and disappeared into the Columbia River. Both happened at night. Both drivers had been drinking, both died and both ruined our Christmas.

On one of these occasions we placed a tow truck sideways on the ferry, moved the ferry out to mid-stream, let out the truck's cable and allowed the current to move us back and forth until we found the submerged vehicle. Then, with the assistance of two river men, we began the recovery by using grappling hooks to snag some part of the vehicle. Once snagged we would take up the slack on the tow cable and move the ferry, the tow truck, and the submerged vehicle, inch by inch towards the shore. Repeatedly the grappling hook would come loose and the procedure would start again. Ten hours later, cold and exhausted we landed the vehicle on the shore with the deceased still floating in the back window. We removed him from the vehicle and sat him down beside us at a small camp fire we had kindled on the shoreline. The Coroner had been contacted and a hearse was on its way to remove the body.

An American motorist, who had been waiting for the ferry for several hours, came over and said sympathetically,

You fellas look like you could use a drink.

He handed us a bottle of rum and wished us a Merry Christmas. But our Christmas wasn't to become merry anytime soon, for just when we thought our disappointments were over another motorist arrived at the scene and seeing us sitting at the campfire with the dead man shyly asked if we just might be waiting for a hearse.

Because, if you are, he said, *it's not coming, it's in the ditch about ten miles back and the driver is drunk.*

It was the last straw for Corporal Zaharia, whose wife was still waiting Christmas dinner for our tired and beleaguered crew. So with the coroner's permission we put the dead man in the trunk of our police car, drove to Fred's house, and ate our Christmas dinner. It was midnight. The delivery of the deceased could wait.

With the coming of spring I soon forgot about the hazards of snow slides and the icy roads of the Roger's Pass. Avalanches were the last thing on my mind that day as I patrolled south of Revelstoke on the winding road that led to the Arrowhead lakes country. But on a warm spring day the thoughts of winter and its related problems seemed a million miles away and a lazy drive south was a refreshing break from the hustle and bustle of the main highway. As I slowly wound my way south I noticed in my rear view mirror that another vehicle was making the same trek. It was probably a quarter to half a mile behind and seemed to be maintaining a constant distance.

I happened to cross slowly over a wooden bridge and noticing the rippling water I was suddenly overcome with an compelling urge to pull over and take a closer look. I parked my police car and made my way leisurely back to the bridge and stood there passively gazing at the water bubbling beneath it.

Now, I have never been a hunter, a fisherman, or for that matter much of an environmentalist, and my sudden urge to participate in this ritual seemed strangely odd, yet I was constrained to it by what seemed a powerful inward force. I had perhaps been standing there only a few minutes when I heard the car, which had been following me, approaching. As it slowly crossed behind me on the bridge force of habit caused me to glance to my right as I watched it pass. And then it happened –

the entire rock face of a cliff which bordered the roadway gave way and huge clouds of rock dust suddenly rose to obscure my vision of the parked police car and the vehicle which had just passed it. Years later the sight of the cloud that rose from the 9-11 terrorist attack in New York city brought back the strange sight. And yet, notwithstanding its similarity, it was also strikingly different, for the dust and the smell was a strangely fresh and humid mixture, totally in contrast to the concrete, chocking dust of 9-11.

I immediately assumed both vehicles had been crushed beneath tons of rock and I sprinted into the cloud in the hope of finding the unsuspecting motorist. The police car stood intact and just beyond it, the passing vehicle. It stood with its front bumper up against a wall of rock that must have stood forty of fifty feet high. The driver sat behind the wheel frozen in time. I ran to his side. The driver's side window was down I spoke to him. There was no response. I opened the door, reached in and tried to help him from the vehicle – but his hands were welded to the wheel. I pried his fingers open one-by-one before the shock of his ordeal began to wear off enough for him to regain his composure and allow me to assist him from the vehicle.

It took only a few more minutes before I began to realize that about a mile of highway had been buried by the slide and I came to the startling conclusion – that had I not stopped to look at that babbling brook – I would have been buried beneath it. Some of my fellow officers said it was my *Karma*, others called it was just *plain luck*; it would be years before I would finally come to understand that something more was at work.

The winter months provided a plethora of crashes to investigate but sometimes the sudden snowfalls of early spring could extend winter's grip and produce havoc on the pass. Such was the case on a beautiful Easter long weekend. The weather had been unusually warm, the roadway was clear and dry and travellers made their way across the pass with little or no effort. From Friday to Sunday the positive weather system remained, but on Monday, the final day of the long weekend, heavy wet snow blanketed the pass and trapped many motorists unfamiliar with the dangers of mountain driving in winter conditions.

It was a six AM start for me on the that Easter Monday and twelve hours later I would have driven a mere forty-five miles to the summit of the Roger's Pass and back – simply investigating accidents along the way. I don't recall most of them, but one in particular I shall never forget.

It was on my return trip, early in the afternoon, at the top of the Albert Canyon Hill. I came upon three vehicles littering the highway. Although traffic could gingerly weave its way through the scene, the vehicles were heavily damaged and required tow truck assistance. But the more pressing problem was that six people were injured and an ambulance was urgently required. Unfortunately, at that time, the city of Revelstoke only had one ambulance and that was a jeep that could only carry a maximum of two people. It was a regular occurrence therefore to solicit the help of passing motorists, particularly people with station wagons to assist in carrying the injured to the Revelstoke hospital.

Having assessed the situation I made my way back to my patrol car to radio for the ambulance and tow trucks. I had parked the car off the travel portion of the highway on the shoulder of the roadway with its dome light flashing, but the road conditions were poor and the low hanging cloud made visibility limited.

As was my habit I only partially entered the police car, sitting on the driver's seat, leaning over to grab the radio, and resting the driver's door against my left leg. I made the radio connection to the Revelstoke detachment and was making my requests when I glanced into the rear view mirror and saw a vehicle rapidly approaching. The female driver had lost control and the vehicle was heading directly for the police car. There was no time to react. It was one of those moments when time moves in freeze frame proportion, when split seconds are immeasurably stretched, and a surreal slow motion plays out in which only fate determines the final outcome.

Remarkably, a direct impact was avoided, but the uninhibited vehicle caught the driver's door of the police car and bent it backwards against the cruiser's front left quarter panel, passing over my leg effectively trapping me between the two vehicles. It was one of those times when you pause a few seconds to see if you're going to suddenly feel the pain. I was already physically exhausted, now I was suddenly filled with anger. I glared over at the driver and her male passenger, now so close that I could reach over and touch him, and I angrily hollered, *"Back up!"* The driver burst into tears and for the first time in my life I felt like pulling out my gun and shooting someone. Maybe she recognized the intent in my eyes because she suddenly regained her composure, put the vehicle in reverse and slowly backed away.

My leg was free and although my pants had been torn and I had some soreness it appeared I was not seriously injured. Thankfully, I was able to limp about the accident scene attending to those who were injured and completing my investigation. Perhaps it was my desire to avoid the barrage of paperwork in reporting police car accidents, or maybe the fact that one of the tow truck operators at the scene offered to fix the damaged patrol car for just a few dollars that caused me to let the young lady go with a warning to drive more carefully, but that's what I did. My leg was merely bruised, the damage could be easily repaired, and the day was finally over. Of course I'll never forget it, but then I don't suppose she will either.

19
Highway Patrol Nightmares

Revelstoke highway patrol duties ranged from shear boredom to heart pounding trepidation. Accidents in mountainous terrain can be spectacular and in those days officers were obliged to use their ingenuity at almost every crash scene. Resources were limited. Radio contact could be non-existent in some areas requiring the conscription of passing motorists to courier messages for tow trucks and ambulances. Truckers were often an officer's best friends, particularly during winter months, and on many occasions I solicited their cooperation to pull vehicles from dangerous positions or assist in freeing trapped drivers.

One such incident occurred just a few miles West of Revelstoke at a place called Summit Lake. A semi-trailer truck had left the road and crashed head-on into a large boulder. The severity of the impact caused its load of steel rods to slide forward pinning the driver's lower body in the cab of the tractor. When I arrived I found the driver alert but with the lower part of his body held securely by the load of steel.

The problem was that even though I had an ambulance standing by, the only tow truck available was unable to budge the load in order to release the trapped trucker. As I pondered the situation I had a chat with the driver and he told me he had struck a rock on the roadway which caused him to loose control. Unfortunately, the physical evidence did not support his claim and the curve of the road where the accident occurred suggested he had simply missed the curved and driven into the rock at highway speed. I returned to the cab to question him a little more. I told him he was liar, he didn't respond, but neither could he look me in the eye. Sadly, at that moment neither of us knew just how serious his condition really was.

As I mused over what might be done several more truckers arrived at the scene. Truckers were always willing helpers and I always appreciated their knowledge and expertise. Discussing the situation with them we jointly surmised that if we couldn't pull the load from its position, we might at least tip it over and rescue the driver.

It took us about an hour and in the process we utilized four semi-trailer tractors and a Department of Highways grader to execute our plan. Each participating unit was attached by a cables to the disabled unit and then, when the slack was individually taken up from each connecting cable, I gave the signal for the collective effort to begin. The strain on the cables was worrisome. I had seen tow cables snap before when trying to lift vehicles from mountainous terrain. A snapped cable flies through the air like a metal whip and can easily decapitate an unsuspecting individual. But the cables held and the steel laden trailer began to lose its grip on the boulder. It teetered and rocked until the right side wheels lifted from the ground and it toppled over onto its left side.

As the cables slacked I ran to the cab and reached in to pull the driver free. He had lost consciousness. As I reached under the remaining debris to free the lower half of his body I felt a sinking feeling in the depths of my soul. Everything from the waist down had a pillow like softness and I knew he must have been completely crushed. As others assisted me in pulling him free his foot detached from his body and remained in my hand. I knew at that moment he was going to die and I was sorry for how abrupt I had been with him in our conversation.

Police officers can become very hardened and bitter by the things they see and the events in which they participate. Inwardly, I suspect it's a coping mechanism more than anything else, otherwise one could hardly expect to maintain sanity. I have often shared with doctors, nurses, soldiers and firemen, who have experienced similar reactions, sometimes even turning to humour in moments that would otherwise turn stomachs. That's why it is so unfair for those who have never experienced such trauma to sit back in some council or courtroom months, or even years later, and question the actions of those who have confronted these issues *face to face* and in *real time*.

Final investigations corroborated my theory – the deceased had pushed his luck for months driving from Edmonton to Vancouver and return – alone and non-stop, a total distance of 2488 kilometres. He had refused to have a companion driver – twice the miles; half the help, equals twice the money. To cope with the long hours he had resorted to taking *stay awake* pills. I guess the body can only take so much; there was little doubt that he simply dozed off – perhaps just long enough to miss that fateful curve near Summit Lake. I haven't been past there in many years, but I suspect that boulder is still there.

Members on highway patrol are exposed to a large number of crashes every year and in the early 1960's with limited resources available officers often had to use their own ingenuity to resolve difficult situations. One such case simply began when I noticed a portion of curbing missing on a curve portion of highway overlooking the fast flowing Illecillewaet River. When I stopped to investigate I could see a vehicle half submerged in the water below. I took a rope from the trunk of the police car, tied it under the frame and descended the embankment, but the fast moving waters prevented me from getting any closer to the vehicle and although I doubted anyone was still trapped inside I could not confirm that fact.

Fortunately, as traffic began to slow and gawkers began to accumulate I was approached by two men who were scuba divers from the Calgary area and happened to have their equipment with them in the vehicle. So, telling them that I had no idea if I could actually pay them for their services, but assuring them I would try, I asked if they would be willing to assist me. They were happy to oblige, they donned their wet suits descended the embankment, entered the rushing waters and searched the vehicle. There was no evidence of anyone inside. Thoughtfully, they stood by until a tow truck arrived and helped to attach its cables in order that the vehicle might be removed. I recorded their names, thanked them and eventually did get the government to pay each of them fifty dollars for searching the vehicle. But my problems had just begun, the registration indicated the driver was a young man from Revelstoke who was heading to the Glacier area for work – now he was missing and obviously presumed drowned. But where was the body?

The Illecillewaet River flows with vigour winding between the highway and the rail line that crisscross its domain. A search along the highway portion of the river proved futile, but I knew there were portions of the rail line that bordered the river that were unobservable and inaccessible from the highway. So I contacted Cst. Don McEachern of the Canadian Pacific Railway police for his assistance and a plan was formulated to further extend the search for the missing man.

First, since there was only one rail line running through the pass all train traffic would have to be stopped for a certain period of time – they granted us four hours. Secondly, we would take a small powered track vehicle, commonly known as a jigger, and travel along the track from Revelstoke to the Albert Canyon and back. That would allow us to double check the area where the body would have passed. Of course, we knew that nothing could have prevented the body from eventually flowing over the Revelstoke power dam located just a few more miles downstream, in which case we would probably never find it.

So we donned work clothes, strapped on our guns and police hats, packed our lunch, some lengths of rope, two sets of binoculars, and made off on our jigger. Now, I have never been one to enjoy heights, in fact, I am quite afraid of them and crossing railway trestles on an open air jigger, without side rails was for me quite an experience. But each time we would come in sight of the river we would stop and survey it with our binoculars.

We had departed about 8:00AM and by about 10:00 we had found our target. Viewed through the binoculars the body could be seen at a curve on the opposite side of the river and it appeared as though it had become entangled in the roots and branches from an overturned tree trunk. Unfortunately, the body was completely inaccessible from our side of the river, so we took bearings as best we could and decided our best bet was to continue on the rail line until we came somewhere close to the highway, then hitchhike back to the general area and try to reach it from the highway side of the river.

When we reached within striking distance of the highway we pulled the jigger from the track and flagged down a passing motorist. Needless to say they were somewhat sceptical of the two vagabonds they were picking up, but they dropped us off as requested and since we had no radio contact we asked them to inform the RCMP detachment in Revelstoke of our location.

Then we began to negotiate the wilderness area between the highway and the river, keeping in mind the bearings that would bring us somewhere in the vicinity of the deceased. But the going was difficult and in places we had to balance on fallen tree trunks across fast raging water, like tightrope walkers with our hands stretched outward to maintain our balance. With the depth and swiftness of the water a false step would likely have meant certain death. Yet even as we inched our way forward we recognized the fact that we would never be able to bring the body back by the same route.

Thirty minutes later we found him, still clinging to the undergrowth of an uprooted tree. He was a big lad, probably weighing two hundred and fifty pounds. His size only added to our dilemma. We sat down beside him, ate our lunch and pondered the situation. It would soon be getting dark; if something was to be done it had to be done quickly.

At this location the river made a sharp right curve and in about a quarter of a mile another abrupt turn this time to the left, but in doing so it came within a stone's throw of the highway. Now a thought came to mind. If a person were careful enough and perhaps just a bit lucky they might be able to make their way along the river bank to the spot near the highway. But the bank was certainly not wide enough to allow us to carry the body and we were afraid to leave it unless it broke free and continued on towards the dam.

Then we made a difficult decision. Since all we had with us was a rope, we would tie the body securely to one end, then wind the other end around our waists and float the body downstream while we attempted to make our way along the shoreline. When all was set we looked hopefully at each other and unhooked the body from its snagged position. We didn't have to wait long to see if our idea would work, the current snatched the body from our grasp and began to move it rapidly down stream. Furiously, we scrambled along the river's edge, hanging on for dear life and hoping the weight of the body would not pull us both into the river with him. We stumbled and sprinted along the shoreline and in minutes reached the curve near the highway. Frantically, we used all of our strength to pull the deceased from the water and flopped down beside him exhausted and very, very grateful.

It's strange how at times when you are in the presence of the dead you can sometimes find yourself talking to them, even as you talk to a friend. It was like we had helped a long time friend bring an end to a difficult experience. I think all three of us were glad it was over.

20

Wyatt Earp Syndrome

Even though police officers are sometimes delegated to specific duties like the enforcement of traffic laws it never relieves them of their responsibility to assist in a variety of other policing issues and for that reason officers can find themselves in a variety of investigations and surprisingly dangerous predicaments.

Two of my uncles were city police officers in Regina, Saskatchewan. One, while on motorcycle traffic duties pulled over a car that failed to stop at a red light. As he walked up to the vehicle the driver raised his hands to surrender. Beside him on the seat were a revolver and a bag of money from the bank he had just robbed. Jimmy Halpenny was lucky that day. More than one police officer has been killed when unsuspectingly walking into a dangerous situation. Familiarity for police officers really does breed contempt and is a very real and constant danger. It's when an officer lays down his guard thinking he's making just another routine traffic stop or attending another unresolvable family feud that he becomes the most vulnerable. I must admit that I have fallen into that trap myself on more than one occasion.

In fact, one incident immediately comes to mind. I was patrolling in the city of Revelstoke when I overheard a radio call for police attendance at a fight in progress at a local rooming house. I was just three blocks from the scene and I volunteered to respond. As I pulled up in front of the run down two story house I could hear the sounds of a disturbance within. As I exited the car a crashing sound caused me to look up. It was akin to a scene from an old western movie, the upper torso of a man came smashing through an upper window sending glass shattering to the street below. Only the combatant's quick reaction in grabbing the outside of the window frame with outstretched arms prevented his plummeting to the ground. Then, with only the slightest hesitation he launched himself back into the room and rejoined the fray.

I arrived first and entered the building cautiously, allowing time for backup officers to arrive on the scene. As two arrived I entered the lower floor and hesitated again before ascending the staircase to the second floor fight scene. There were four combatants in the room and our arrival brought things to a sudden halt. A breeze through the broken window caused the curtain over a hot plate to ignite in flame. It was quickly torn from its supporting rod and stamped out on the floor. Blood was everywhere. One man's thumb was the source of the bloodletting and remained attached by only a thin layer of skin. It was then that Cst. Benn noticed blood smears on a bed spread where someone had hastily wiped the blood from a knife. Immediately he asked,

"Who's got the knife?"

There was no answer. Then I heard a hand slap against the leather of a holster and saw Cst. Benn, his hand on his weapon say,

"Don't even think about it."

I looked behind me and saw that one of the men had reached out onto the roof and retrieved the knife – he was standing at my back with a hateful look in his eyes. He dropped the knife and I realized then that Gordie Benn may well have saved my life.

Forrest Gump's mother always told him that *"Stupid is as stupid does."* And boy was she right, I have done some stupid things in my life and that surely ranked with the best of them. A police officer should never let anyone get behind them in a situation like that. Maybe that's why even now, these many years later, I prefer to sit in a restaurant with my back to the wall. It must be some kind of *Wyatt Earp syndrome*.

21
Marble Game Madness

It's a sad fact that the marriages of many police officers fail and while the reasons are no doubt multifaceted some are undoubtedly linked to the strains of police work. It seems the harsh realities experienced in the performance of such duties simply cannot be completely comprehended by a marriage partner no matter how close they believe themselves to be.

To complicate matters, at least in the marriages of RCMP officers, initial postings are often hundreds, if not thousands of miles from extended family and long time friends. Subsequently, when newly married couples experience the growing pains of married life there is no support network available for them to draw upon. Ironically, however, this situation can also work to strengthen a marriage by compelling the partners to rely more heavily upon one another.

It was that kind of perseverance that Gail and I applied to our marriage and the birth of our son, Bret, in Revelstoke on December 3rd, 1967 strengthened our marriage. Yet, even that might not have been enough had it not been for other officers, their wives and newly formed friends from within the communities in which we lived, who often provided us with good counsel and lifelong friendships. Every city and every posting added to our Christmas card list and while it is impossible to mention every one of them perhaps none were so essential as those we came to know in our first posting in Revelstoke, B.C. Carl Gunderson, John and Karen Delano, Len and Marlene Grinnell and Rollie and Wanda Hollowaty who introduced us to our first *marble game*.

If there is one thing a highway patrolman can't do without it is gas and that was where I first met a character named Rollie. Rollie was a gas station attendant and every day during my years of service on the Roger's Pass highway patrol I would either begin or end my day in a face to face with Rollie. We hit it off immediately and I say he was a character because there are only a handful of people you meet in your life that might be truly described in that manner.

A *character* is one of those unique individuals, who can best be described as *other*, because no matter who else you try to compare them with, they are simply *other* than that – characters are one of a kind and Rollie was and still is one.

It was Rollie and Johnnie Delano that taught me to laugh at myself. We were like the three stooges racing down Mt. Mackenzie Ski Hill with little or no idea how to ski and even less idea on how to stop - crashing into the towrope building and rolling in the snow in side splitting laughter. Sometimes, while on patrol I would see Rollie walking down the street, jump out of the police car and run over to him. Suddenly, he'd turn and fight. We'd tussle right there on main street until I'd finally toss him into the back seat of the police car. Then I'd hop back into the driver's seat and race off as if I had just arrested Revelstoke's most violent offender. In a block or two I'd pull over and we'd share a very healthy laugh.

Rollie and Wanda and their two children lived in an apartment above the National Parks offices and supplemented their income by cleaning the building every night. Sometimes Gail and I would lend a hand and afterward we would retire to their apartment for an evening of great friendship. We'd put our son Bret down to sleep amidst a bundle of blankets in their bathtub and enjoy their fellowship until the wee small hours of the morning.

On the occasional Friday or Saturday night I had off Gail and Wanda would visit, while Rollie and I would sit outside on the ledge that surrounded the upper floor of the building. From that vantage point we could easily watch the shenanigans that inevitably took place on the street below. In fact, I still smile when I recall watching one of the Norberg boys parade down Revelstoke's main streets at 3 o'clock in the morning playing his bagpipes. He walked alone down the middle of the street and when he reached an intersection he would make a smart military type turn and march off down the next street. The amusing thing was that a police car was slowly patrolling street by street looking for this mystery piper and from our vantage point we could easily watch both participants in this rather unusual dance for no matter which way the police car turned the piper turned in another direction. The officers could obviously hear the bagpipes but they never did find that lone Norberg piper.

It was on one of these sanity satisfying visits with our friends the Hollowatys that we were introduced to the *marble game*. In some ways it was just a variation of a game called *Sorry*, but with a few variations that made it a lot more fun. Rollie had even made his own colour-coded game board from a piece of plywood. Anyway, since the game was best played in teams a vigorous rivalry soon developed between the men and the ladies. Generally, but not always – the men won. But the frivolity that took place during these classic tournaments was the best therapy a young police officer and a young married couple could ever have received. All things considered, it was probably *marble game madness* that prevented the insanity of at least this one police officer.

22

A Queen Charlotte Logger

When I arrived at the RCMP Detachment in Revelstoke I was introduced to Corporal Vern Meyers. Vern was six foot six – a mountain of a man, but his statute was dwarfed by his sense of humor. Vern was a practical joker of the first order. It was to be expected then that a rookie like me would be a prime target for one of Vern's misdemeanors.

It happened on a beautiful summer night. Cpl. Meyers decided he would go out on patrol with me in a supervisory capacity. As we made our way down Victoria Road we found ourselves following an old blue panel truck and Cpl. Meyers decided I should pull this vehicle over and check its taillights. Little did I know at the time that it was one of Vern's practical jokes. He knew very well who was driving that old truck and what I was about to get myself into.

When I approached the driver's door a friendly smile greeted me and the driver opened the conversation saying,

Good evening, officer, what seems to be the trouble?

I told him I would like to see his driver's license and I would like to take a look at his taillights. To which he enthusiastically replied,

No problem, I'm a Queen Charlotte logger and I been driving these big rigs for thirty years, got receipts for everything!

With that introduction he leaned over and pulled out a shoe box stuffed to overflowing with receipts of every kind and color, hopped out of his vehicle and began to lay each one out on the hood of his vehicle, being careful with each receipt to tell me precisely what it was for and when he had received it. One glance back at the police car told the story. Vern was beside himself with laughter. He had known old Chapman for many years and as harmless as he was he could easily fill an hour with meaningless conversation. Fortunately, for me I managed to pry myself loose after about forty minutes. Vern thought it might even be a new record. It seemed every new officer arriving at the detachment had to be introduced to Revelstoke's Queen Charlotte logger.

A good sense of humor can easily be a police officer's best friend and two years later, on a cold winter's night, I found myself on highway patrol West of Revelstoke. Near a place called Summit Lake I came upon a stranded motorist. His car had broken down and I stopped to ask if he needed any assistance. He told me everything was looked after. I asked if he was absolutely certain, since I probably wouldn't be back that way for several hours and the blustery weather was anything but accommodating. He assured me again that he was alright and I continued my patrol.

About three hours later I rounded the curve to Summit Lake and there he was my stranded motorist, flagging me down and desperately trying to warm himself by jumping up and down. Eagerly, he jumped into the police car and helped himself to the heater's output. When he had a moment to thaw himself out and collect his thoughts I asked,

What happened, I thought you said you had help on the way?

He replied,

Well, I thought I did, this guy came by, he stopped and told me he had all the equipment I needed in Revelstoke – even owned his own wrecker – said he would go get it and be right back for me. But I haven't seen him since.

I hesitated a moment, then asked,

What exactly was this fellow driving?

His reply brought a smile to my face.

He was driving an old blue panel truck – said his name was Chapman.

I couldn't help but chuckle; it seemed my stranded motorist had been personally introduced to Revelstoke's Queen Charlotte logger.

23
Burning Questions

In mountainous regions fire can be one of a patrolman's worst enemies. Wilderness areas provide little or no access to fire fighting equipment and where it is available it often requires water to be pumped from nearby streams or rivers. Unfortunately, with the onset of winter many such water sources are frozen and inaccessible.

I had three experiences with vehicle fires and each came with its own unique lesson. The first began as a small fire in a mobile home being towed across the Roger's Pass during the winter months. The driver detected smoke seeping from the undercarriage of the unit and called for assistance from the National Parks service which regrettably was unable to help because of the weather. Even attempts by the driver and myself to chop out the smoldering area with a hatchet failed, and sadly, I sat in my patrol car throughout the night and watched a fully furnished mobile home go up in smoke with only the periodic explosion of the tires keeping me awake. Lesson one – *even the seemingly smallest fire can still beat you.*

Lesson two also came on a cold night in January. It was four o'clock in the afternoon, my shift was about finished and I was just two miles from Revelstoke when I received a call to attend an accident just a few miles back down the road I had just traversed. When I turned around I could see a column of smoke rising into the sky and knew it was serious.

The accident had taken place on a bridge deck. A truck pulling the first section of a double wide mobile home had pulled over to its right to make room for a logging truck passing in the opposite direction. Unfortunately, a corner of the mobile home caught the edge of the bridge abutment causing the unit to jack knife in the middle of the bridge. At the same time, a second truck pulling the second half of the mobile home, plowed into the back of the first. While the logging truck escaped contact both housing units burst into flames completely blocked the bridge in both directions.

Having established that no one was trapped in the burning vehicles and knowing that no firefighting equipment was available there was little left to do but watch the units burn and since the fire was intense everything on the bridge deck was reduced to rubble within about five hours.

When I could finally make my way onto the bridge deck I conducted my investigation as quickly as possible in order that efforts could be made to reopen the highway but as yet I had no idea of just how I might accomplish that task. The miles of frustrated motorists that met me on the opposite side of the bridge shared my dilemma and no one could present any viable options.

It was then that I spotted a D9 Caterpillar on a flat bed truck near the front of the line. I asked the driver of the rig if perchance he could operate the cat on the back of his truck. When he answered affirmatively, I asked if he would like to use it to clear the bridge. His smile lit up the night sky. When he fired up that caterpillar a cheer went up from the stalled motorists, but an insurance agent on the scene approached and asked if I was really serious, after all he had not yet finished his investigation. I told him if he didn't want to get run over he'd better get out of the way. In minutes the bridge was cleared and the Trans-Canada highway was open again. Lesson two – *when the fire's out get the traffic moving.*

Lesson three was by far the most difficult and yet it took place on a mild summer's night and with the Revelstoke Fire Department in attendance. The instance unfolded with a report of a car on fire near the on-ramp of the Trans-Canada Highway. At this time the Revelstoke Fire Department was primarily a volunteer group with only a few full time members. When emergencies took place an audible horn would sound throughout the city and the volunteers would either drive to the station or follow the fire truck to the scene. What complicated the matter on this occasion was that a local carnival was being celebrated in the city and some of the volunteers were participating in the festivities. Bert Bradstock was dressed as a clown; his face was covered with cotton batten to simulate a full beard.

When I arrived at the scene I saw a vehicle on the North side of the highway completely engulfed in flames. A fire truck was on the scene and several firefighters including Bradstock were actively endeavoring to extinguish it. Another officer had also just arrived from the opposite direction. Then, as I pulled up to the scene, the burning car exploded. Flames shot across the hood of my police car and I instinctively dove down across the front seat even as I hit the brakes. For an instant I thought my own car would ignite, but it was merely the flash from the explosion. As I hastily exited the police car a dreadful sight flooded my vision. The other officer was on his hands and knees over the prone body of Bert Bradstock and attempting to extinguish the blazing cotton batten on Bert's face with his bare hands.

Bert's body was badly burned and within a few hours I attended with Corporal Vern Meyers at the Revelstoke Hospital. Vern had the same blood type as Bert and had volunteered to provide blood. That's when Revelstoke's most notoriously incompetent doctor made another of his incredulous blunders. While intending to take a vial of blood from Vern Dr. Armstrong inadvertently failed to push the plunger down on the syringe, which of course would have drained the air from within it, instead he put the syringe into Vern's arm, pushed the plunger down and injected the air directly into his vein. Instantly, Corporal Meyers looked at Armstrong and said,

Did you just inject air into my arm? Isn't that the way they sometimes kill people?

And Armstrong in his usual adept beside manner replied,

Well, we'll know in a minute or two!

Immediately Corporal Meyers instructed me to begin making notes of what had just taken place and the resulting conversation. Already he was beginning to feel light-headed and unsteady on his feet. Fortunately, Meyers was a big man standing six foot six and probably weighing at least two hundred and fifty pounds. It was his size that most likely saved his life and although he later underwent a battery of tests at Vancouver General Hospital he suffered no lasting effects from the incident. Sadly, notwithstanding Vern's sacrifice and his blood transfusion Bert Bradstock died a few days later.

Lesson three had two parts. Part one – *When a car is on fire and no one is inside, just stand back and let it burn.* Bert Bradstock had lost his life needlessly. Part two – *incompetent doctors sometimes hide out in small towns.*

24
For Pleasure Go Greyhound

Although you would think there would be fewer accidents on the Roger's Pass during the summer months the increase in tourist traffic actually swelled the crash ratio. And while weather conditions were much less likely to be contributing factors, dry roads prompted drivers to increase speed and take even greater risks.

Strangely the damage incurred in crashes was often disproportionate to the injuries sustained. For example, a fourteen year old girl lost control of a stolen car, rolled it a number of times down a two hundred foot embankment flattening it to half its original height, and walked away unscathed, while a middle aged driver experienced a flat tire which pulled his vehicle sharply to the right causing it to come in contact with a rock bluff. The vehicle sustained negligible damage and yet his mother, who was sitting in the passenger seat, struck her head on the dashboard and was killed instantly. Unfortunately, seat belts were not mandatory in the early 1960's and the lap belts surfacing in newer vehicles were seldom used. But there is no doubt that some of the major injuries sustained in seemingly minor collisions would have been much less severe if seat belts had been readily available and actively employed.

But seat belts have never been mandatory on buses, neither have bus transportation companies such as Greyhound ever been required to maintain manifests listing the passengers on board. Now while that may seem trivial to most people, any emergency personnel who have ever attended a major bus accident can tell you that bodies fly from one end of the bus to the other and in some cases are thrown completely out of the bus. In addition, severely injured people and obviously those who are dead cannot tell you who they are or who their next of kin might be, a problem that is only magnified when dealing with female passengers who seldom carry identification on their person. Women tend to carry their personal papers in a purse or a carry-on bag from which they are easily separated on impact. On the other hand, men usually carry wallets in their pockets so can generally be more rapidly identified.

The lack of a passenger manifest, such as required when traveling on ships and aircraft also means that, with the exception of tour buses, no one really knows exactly who is travelling on any bus at any particular time. Passengers may also embark and disembark at any of the stops along a designated route which may reduce or add to the original passenger grouping.

If these conditions were not imposing enough the bus crash that took place at Glacier, B.C. saw five people killed and forty-five injured at a location serviced by only two ambulances, one from Revelstoke and one from Golden, B.C. cities, each located some forty-five miles from the crash site.

Road construction was in progress in the area at the time of the collision and crews had just placed a tacky surface coating on the highway in preparation for repaving when a sudden cloud burst made the road surface extremely slippery. The driver of the Greyhound bus, which was travelling East at the time, had pulled the bus over to the right shoulder of the road and was proceeding cautiously uphill through the construction zone. Unfortunately, a gravel truck travelling in the opposite direction lost control on the slippery surface and collided broadside with the front of the bus.

The impact virtually wrapped the truck around the front end of the bus killing the driver and the several passengers in the neighbouring front seats.

I was not the first to arrive on the scene, in fact, I was off duty and called to come in urgently and transport Dr. Hamer from Revelstoke to the scene. There were no such things as Air Ambulances available in those days and the limited number of ground ambulances meant that many of the injured were going to have an extended wait before they could be transported to hospital.

When we arrived at the scene it reminded me of one of the scenes from the nightly newsreels on CBS reporting on the Vietnam War. The ditch was lined with bodies, some were obviously dead, others badly injured. A number of people were milling about, staggering in various states of shock. An old man approached me, asked me where he could find his wife and then collapsed into my arms. As I tried to console him he died there in my arms. I laid him gently down at the roadside and helped Dr. Hamer climb into the bus through a broken window. The gravel truck wrapped around the front of the bus prevented access through the front door, a number of passengers were trapped inside and Dr. Hamer wanted to get to them as quickly as possible. It was a scene I will never forget.

With only two ambulances relaying the injured we commandeered passing vehicles to assist in the evacuation. The accident occurred at about eleven o'clock in the morning but the turmoil did not end much before three or four in the afternoon. Only then could the actual investigation of the collision begin.

We requested that both the truck and the bus be taken to Revelstoke, B.C. where mechanical inspections could be performed, but political pressure applied by the bus company resulted in the bus being towed instead to Golden. It was the first time in my career when I was a witness to political interference overriding common sense. Greyhound wanted to examine the bus at their own facility which seemed to me to apply a rather biased overtone to the investigation. Although it seemed clear that the trucker had been primarily responsible and that the bus driver had done everything he could to avoid the crash, in my opinion, an objective investigation had clearly been compromised.

I was still at the scene later that evening when the first representatives of Greyhound arrived. They brought along their own work crew who covered the front of the bus with a tarp and then spray painted the bus grey to camouflage it from passing motorists and hide the slogan which ran down the outside length of the bus and read,

For pleasure go Greyhound.

At 1AM I finally pulled the covers over my head and went to sleep. At 2AM the telephone rang and an hour later I could hardly believe I was on the road again this time to an occurrence a few miles south of Revelstoke. Two vehicles carrying a number of young people had been drag racing down the deserted southern highway, apparently neither was prepared to *chicken out* at the curve that rapidly approached and both ran head-on into the mountainside.

Michael White was a passenger in a convertible. The top was down and when they struck the embankment Michael's head was impaled on the door frame on the right side of the front windshield. I had to take him by the hair to pull his head from its position. His eyes were wide open and you didn't have to be a doctor to know that Micheal was dead.

Michael had been a trouble maker and a continuous annoyance to the local detachment for years, yet still it was not the kind of death anyone would have wished even for him. Today my memory fails me as to whether there were two who died that night or just Michael, perhaps it is just the body's way of coping I don't know, after all whether it was six or seven dead within that sixteen hours didn't really seem to matter. I was beginning to feel like I was in my own version of Vietnam.

25

In Hot Pursuit

To pursue or not pursue a fleeing vehicle is a question which every police officer will likely face sometime in their career and which unfortunately must be answered in a split second. In the first place failing to pursue a fleeing vehicle may allow a dangerous criminal to escape capture. Imagine for a moment, being a hostage held in such a vehicle, and then having the pursuing police officer break off the pursuit leaving you in the hands of what might well be your executioner. Secondly, abandoning pursuits encourages others to attempt similar methods in order to evade apprehension. So, impaired drivers, people driving after their licences have been suspended and in some cases even those trying to avoid responsibility for minor motor vehicle infractions like speeding are encouraged to *make a run for it.*

But high speed pursuits can be deadly, not only for those fleeing or pursuing, but also for innocent bystanders and unsuspecting motorists. It's a question not easily answered and often criticized by lawyers and judges who have had the added convenience of months to reflect upon the decision. The lack of support for officers faced with such momentary decisions is nothing short of contemptible and certainly does nothing to support officers faced with these tough choices.

Having been involved in a number of high speed chases I can testify to the difficulty officers face in making such determinations. On one occasion I pursued a stolen vehicle some ninety miles on mountain roads from Revelstoke to Golden, B.C. at reckless speeds. The smaller engine in my police car made it impossible for me to overtake the driver of the much more powerful vehicle. I closed rapidly on the vehicle on the curved portions of the canyons with which I was obviously much more familiar, but quickly fell behind on the straight stretches as the vehicle simply walked away from me.

I was accompanied by another officer and recall us both hitting our heads on the roof as our vehicle became airborne on a bridge deck that was under reconstruction. When we entered several snowsheds I backed off as the fleeing vehicle careened from one side to the other as it negotiated patches of black ice. Vaguely I remember passing a Greyhound bus whose driver later remarked to an officer in Revelstoke,

Well, I thought that first car was moving but boy that police car chasing him was really flying.

The whole pursuit ended near Golden, B.C. with a road block at which point the driver fled from the vehicle into a nearby lumber yard. With guns drawn and nerves frayed officers searched relentlessly until they finally located the suspect hiding behind a stack of two by fours. He was a fourteen year old boy who had escaped from a youth detention centre in Vancouver. All that trouble and all the collateral danger it had exposed others to had been generated by not much more than a child. Yet one can only imagine the furor that would have erupted if that fourteen year old had been killed in a police chase or perhaps even shot in the heat of the moment.

Anyone who has never been involved in high-speed chase has no idea of the impact such an event makes on the nervous system. The combination of adrenaline, danger and nervous tension can cause emotions to snap like an over tightened guitar string. That's why it's never surprising to me when I see video footage of officers striking out a suspect suddenly apprehended at the end of such an emotionally intensified event. Bystanders, lawyers and judges will simply never be able to comprehend the emotional elements that come into play at such a time.

I tried to reassess every high speed chase I was involved in and many times I realized that choices and decisions I had made were probably not the best. But by reassessing I hoped to make better judgements in the future and I suppose that's really all any officer can do. In any event I knew I would never again chase a vehicle from Revelstoke to Golden. After all there was literally nowhere a fleeing car could escape between the two cities. Ninety miles of mountain highway stretched between the two and there were literally no cross roads. So what was the point? I could just as easily have casually pursued the vehicle from point A to point B without the risk and still have likely accomplished the same purpose with the roadblock at Golden. But youth comes with its own irrationality and it's a lesson that doesn't come easily even to police officers.

Soon however, we began to learn to use even the elements to our advantage in effecting roadblocks and eliminating hot pursuits and since the Revelstoke area was a high snow fall area on several occasions when notified by the Golden detachment that a stolen car was coming over the Roger's Pass, we would simply request assistance from the local Department of Highways. With the use of a grader we could break down the snow banks surrounding the roadway and reform it onto the road in a slowly rising fashion which could not be clearly discerned by the oncoming driver. It was incredibly effective and even amusing to turn on our flashing police car lights only to hear the engine of the oncoming vehicle burst into overdrive as the driver descended the mountain approaching the roadblock. With the police vehicles well off on both sides of the roadway the highway between them appeared wide open and the suspects would invariably take the bait thinking they could easily run the roadblock. But they would soon hit the rising snow pack and no matter how fast the vehicle was travelling it would soon sit stationery and suspended in about four feet of packed snow. It was Mother Nature's perfect roadblock.

Interestingly, the most *fun* I ever had at a roadblock also took place at Golden, B.C. and coincided perfectly with a series of highway patrol road checks that were taking place in the interior of British Columbia. Since most small towns had only one or two highway patrol officers, occasionally our Division Headquarters would devise roving patrols in which officers from a number of detachments would travel from one community to another setting up a series of road checks during which they would thoroughly check drivers for valid licenses, registration and insurance papers and inspect vehicles for faulty equipment. Even large scale commercial trucks were not exempt and since all of us had also been certified in air brake inspection no stone was left unturned.

Now one day one of these roving blitzes just happened to wind up in the town of Golden and since Golden, B.C. is near to the Alberta border we decided to ask the officers from the Alberta area to drop over for a little social interaction and some informational exchanges. So picture this scene. Twelve police officers from British Columbia are sharing a beer and some fellowship with about eight officers from Alberta in my hotel room at a motel situated along side of the Trans Canada Highway. The telephone rings. I answer it and it is the Golden RCMP detachment. The caller is the member on duty at the Golden detachment; he identifies himself and says,

Revelstoke detachment just called and one of their cars is pursuing a stolen car from Revelstoke to Golden. There are apparently four men in it and they are requesting a roadblock, we're short of manpower and we were wondering if there were any members there who might lend a hand?

I could hardly contain myself as I gazed around the room at eighteen or twenty officers. Outside sat at least ten police cars. It must have been the most perfect opportunity ever presented. Of course we agreed to help.

The scene was truly remarkable. Ten police cars at various angles from shoulder to shoulder blocked the highway. Some of which these cruisers were Nash Ramblers, considered to be true pieces of junk, they were therefore placed into the most venerable positions in the hopes that we might get rid of a few. Smaller officers like me were sent to the front ranks knowing full well that the fleeing vehicle would likely get past our first line of defence. Bigger officers were stationed at the rear since they could present a more physical presence when the suspects were confronted. Flares were lit and given to every member to hold with additional flares lining the highway and both adjacent ditches.

Cst. Lud Sterba was driving the pursuing Revelstoke cruiser and since we had loud hailers turned on from our police car radios we could hear his conversation as we saw the suspect vehicle and its pursuing police car top the rise before descending to the roadblock. I'll never forget his words,

Oh my Lord, would you look at that, it looks like a Christmas tree. You can't even see the road it's just lights from one side to the other.

No sooner had he spoken than we heard the fleeing vehicle accelerate at a high rate of speed towards us. Those of us in the front row threw our flares into the windshield as the car sped by somehow, unfortunately, avoiding every Nash Rambler in the process, but coming to a stop exactly where we had intended – adjacent to our biggest and toughest members. It was a scene to warm the cockles of every police officer's heart as four escapees from a prison in the lower mainland were rather roughly arrested as one of them was heard to say,

Son of a ..... we come all the way from Vancouver and never see .... cop then we get to this hick town and there's a bloody hundred of 'em.

It truly was a sweet event.

Winter Patrol Roger's Pass 1965

Winter patrol on the Old Big Bend Highway 1965

Snow slide on the Roger's Pass 1966
Cst. Bob Selwood (left) author (right)

Ferry Crossing Highway 23 South of Revelstoke 1965

Roof of vehicle underwater that left the ferry and
entered the Columbia River on Christmas Eve1965

Recovery boat crew – author (right), Guide - Carl
Gunderson (center) and unidentified boatman (left)

Vehicle being pulled from the Columbia River

Body being recovered from Columbia River
three months after ferry accident. 1966

Missing bridge railing is evidence of an
accident scene. Roger's Pass 1967

Vehicle found below the damaged bridge deck

Vehicle recovered from the Columbia River
Keys found in the ignition. No driver ever located 1967

Semi-trailer truck accident near the summit
of the Roger's Pass during the winter of 1967

Vehicle (arrow) in Illecillewaet River, Albert
Canyon, Roger's Pass. 1967

Close-up of vehicle in Illecillewaet River

Divers hired from amongst passing motorists
to search vehicle in the Illecillewaet River

Police car location (arrow) where my leg was pinned
between a vehicle and the police car in a subsequent accident

Bridge where two trucks pulling house trailers
collided and burned six miles
East of Revelstoke 1967

Rescue workers attempting to free seven people trapped
in a vehicle (before the invention of the *jaws of life*)
near Three Valley Gap, Trans-Canada Highway 1967

A Dominion Bride crane operator assisting in the
removal of a vehicle that left the Old Big Bend Highway
at Silver Creek Falls North of Revelstoke 1966

26
Good Cop/Bad Cop

If Sergeant Smith was the ideal detachment commander and a fine example of a *good cop*, and an excellent manager, his replacement Sergeant Carter was the complete opposite. Carter transferred in to Revelstoke from Prince George, where rumor had it he had no shortage of enemies having apparently betrayed the trust of some of his fellow officers in an internal investigation and although the members of Revelstoke detachment initially welcomed and accepted him it wasn't long before his true character surfaced.

Soon after his arrival he began to freely welcome, and even encourage, the seedier elements of the community into his office where he unequivocally accepted their predominately unfounded complaints against his officers. Of course it didn't take long for these people to realize they could worry him over the slightest   issue and they soon began to manipulate him in various ways.

At the same time he seemed to become more and more paranoid concerning his staff. Perhaps it was the residuum of his dealings in Prince George, but Sgt. Carter trusted no one. Sadly, this lack of trust also caused him to show up at the police office at the strangest of times. Although detachment commanders always worked the day shift it was not unusual for Carter to appear at the office at 7 o'clock in the evening or at 3 o'clock in the morning. He seemed to believe that no one could be trusted to do their job without his direct supervision.

Carter's paranoid expressions even translated to his assessment of his officers and I found myself shaking my head after he completed my annual assessment and told me that although I was one of his best officers he could not possibly put that officially on my service record because his superiors would simply not believe it and they would think he was merely *padding it*.

Then one day he began confronting officers with comments they had made about him – which of course they had made, but which they could not understand how he could possibly know. Understandably, such remarks began to take a toll on the inward trust officers had for one another. Officers began to question whether someone was secretly reporting their confidential conversations. Then one night a shift supervisor happened to need access to Sgt. Carter's office for a particular report and opening the door he discovered a tape deck, with its microphone positioned under the door, recording the conversations taking place in the general office during his absence. Suddenly, the source of the comments became perfectly clear.

Although I didn't particularly like Carter I tried my best to get along with him, after all he was my boss. Then one day it came to a head. It began with an incident that took place while I was simply driving another officer, Cst. Lud Sterba, to work one day. We were driving down the main street in Revelstoke, on a warm spring day on a slush covered road, when I looked into my rear view mirror and noticed a pick up truck following extremely close behind, so close in fact, that I thought if I merely touched my brakes he would surely run into me. I mentioned it to Cst. Sterba and then turned on the dome light of the police cruiser, looked back and pointed for the driver to pull over to the curb.

The driver pulled over. I exited the police car and went back to have a word with him.

During police training officers are instructed never to stop in front of the vehicle they are checking, they are always to park behind, but the circumstances prevented me from doing that and as a result, Cst. Sterba was not able to see what was happening as I checked the vehicle. As I approached the driver got out of the truck and it was rather obvious that he had been drinking. I also noticed there was a small child and a dog in his truck.

Now this was long before the advent of the breathalyzer and in any event I scarcely wanted to arrest this man for impaired driving and have to deal with his child and dog at the same time. So I decided rather to give him a ticket for following too close and a verbal warning about drinking and driving. I asked him to produce his driver's license which he willingly did. But he was clearly becoming more and more agitated as I dealt with him. Then he began to say over and over again, *You have no witnesses, you have no witnesses*. I assumed he was referring to the fact that Cst. Sterba was not witnessing what was taking place. Anyway, I opened my ticket book and the second my pen touched the paper he drove me with a fist to the mouth. The pen and ticket book flew from my hand, my hat flew from my head and my back arched against the hood of the truck preventing me from falling. But since I did not fall down his right cross left him spread across my body and open to a counter-punch. I replied with a left hook to his chin and we both fell into the street locked in the ensuing struggle.

So there we were, thrashing around in the middle of main street, rolling in the slush, throwing wild punches at one another as motorists drove by honking their horns. The honking also seemed to awaken Sterba who embarrassingly came to my aid and assisted in the arrest of the subject, who obviously now had to be arrested for assaulting a police officer. He hit me only three times but he did succeed in breaking my dental plate. He subsequently plead guilty and was fined three hundred dollars.

But the crux of this story is that about two months later the illustrious Sgt. Carter saw this man in a local bar, approached him and asked if he might have a word with him. The subject readily agreed and they moved to a private spot. Then Carter warmly asked,

I was wondering if you could tell me, when you had your confrontation with Dolman, what exactly did he do to provoke you into hitting him?

As the story was later related to me, the subject looked at him, cocked his head to one side, and replied,

Absolutely nothing! It was entirely my fault. But as for you – you can go straight to Hell, because I just don't like you!

With that response my respect for my assailant grew by leaps and bounds and any respect I might have had left for Jim Carter disappeared forever. Sergeant Carter was just a *bad cop*.

27

A Permanent Solution

When my orders came through to transfer from
Revelstoke to Kamloops I had high expectations that conditions
would improve. Policing in a larger city is clearly different than
policing remote highways and the mere fact that backup is readily
available during risky situations is a comfort in itself. However,
being a police officer is not something that can be set aside
during off-duty hours. It's not like working in a retail store where
no one would expect you to serve them after hours. Sooner or
later a police officer will have to deal with the unexpected that
takes place when they are not technically *on duty*.

Al Rabidoux was the manager of the three storey
apartment building Gail and I lived in with our son Bret when we
first arrived in Kamloops in 1968 and he lived with his family in
the house next door. I had met Al on a few occasions and I knew
he had a serious drinking problem. I was involved at that time
with the minor football program in the community and so I also
knew his teenage son who played football for one of the local

bantam teams. He was fine young man who was clearly concerned for his father.

I can't recall just how many times I was summoned to the Rabidoux house to deal with Al, but there were a number of them. I remember one night that I had just come home from work and no sooner sat down to supper when we were interrupted by a loud pounding on our apartment door. It was young David Rabidoux and he was distraught. His father had been drinking again, was seriously depressed, and had gone downstairs with a shotgun intent on killing himself. I had already been over there twice ``that week and although I had no desire to go again I reluctantly went with David.

Al was in the basement with his shotgun and here was I, in uniform and about to descend the staircase to talk to him. I knew very well how many officers are killed in such situations. In fact more officers are killed in domestic disturbances and similar situations than are ever killed in criminal actions. I called out Al, told him who it was, and that I was coming down to talk to him. The truth was I was shaking in my boots. Happily, Al let me descend the stairs and we spent the next few hours reasoning together about life in general. Finally, and perhaps a little reluctantly he put down the gun and came to his senses. As for me, tired and drained, I simply went back to my supper.

My on going relationship with Al continued for a couple of years even after we moved away from the apartment and were living in another part of town and each time the scenario would be the same. He would threaten suicide, we would talk it out, and he would change his mind. Everyone in the detachment knew instinctively that when a call came in concerning Al Rabidoux, I was the one to respond.

Then one day I walked into the office for my first shift after returning from a few weeks holiday and a fellow officer asked,

So did you hear about Al Rabidoux?

I said,

Al, no what about him?

And he replied,

Well, he was arrested for impaired driving. He was asking for you. Someone told him you were away on holidays. They went back a few minutes later and found that he had hung himself in his cell. He's dead.

Even the funeral was over. It was a tough shift for me that night. Even though Al had been a nuisance on many occasions I couldn't help but feel that I had somehow let him down. In fact it would be several years later before I would forgive myself for not having been there for Al when he needed me most.

Unhappily I saw the results of a number of successful suicides during my service and even a few that were not so successful, like the night I responded to a call to find a man using a razor blade on his wrists. He had not only slit his wrists but dug deep holes in each causing them to spray blood like ruptured fire hoses around the room. All I could do was grasp a wrist with each hand, ask someone to drive us to the hospital in the police car, and sit in the back seat with the patient and keep pressure on his wrists.

But more often than not it seemed I was able to talk to people in those circumstances. It was like I could somehow relate to them, perhaps I just did not realize at the time how closely associated I would one day find myself. Deep inside, however, I always realized that suicide was a *permanent solution to a temporary problem.*

28
Life's Fragile Thread

Life is a very precious commodity and sometimes one does not realize just how truly valuable life is until they are in some incident that threatens to end it. Those who have experienced such things will readily confirm that at least two things are common to all such experiences. First, during the actual event time appears to move in slow motion. Split second events seem to require minutes and mere minutes can seemingly drag into hours. Secondly, after the incident has passed troubling revisitations can take place during which the incident is relived again and again, which of course can sometimes cause depression and a condition commonly known as *post traumatic stress disorder*.

But even if serious after effects are not sparked there will inevitably be a series of reevaluations that take place where the situation is thought through repeatedly from various aspects and angles. Those are what I have come to call the *"what ifs"*. *What if* this had happened instead of that? *What if* I had turned left instead of the right? *What if* I hadn't stop to buy a coffee on 42nd Street? Sometimes the *what ifs* can seem never ending. But interestingly, the more one is exposed to life threatening situations and the more *what if* scenarios are encountered the more one begins to believe in karma, fate or some form of divine intervention. Pure chance and luck fall by the wayside because everyone knows that sooner or later your luck simply runs out.

One night as I routinely answered the telephone at the police station in Kamloops I found myself conversing with a distraught man who said he was going to kill someone and needed to talk to someone. Since he was at a nearby hotel barroom and no other officers were immediately available I left the station to meet with him myself, being sure to ask another officer to back me up in case I needed assistance.

I walked into the hotel lobby and as I approached the door that accessed the barroom a man came bursting out, a hunting knife in his hand. I was caught completely unaware. Suddenly, I found myself with a knife leveled at my chest and absolutely no chance to access my revolver which in any event was in a holster covered with a flap. Since I have never considered myself brave I immediately began assessing the scene for any possible means of escape. In front of me was a trembling, knife-wielding man, the door to the barroom on my left, opened outward towards me, effectively eliminating its use. A lobby chesterfield blocked my movement to the right, and in any event two small children sat on it, presumably waiting for their parents. There was simply no where to turn. I was truly trapped. Then, as if to complicate the matter, I saw my back up officer walk by the front door of the hotel obviously thinking I had used another entrance. I would be a liar if I said I wasn't afraid.

I tried to remain calm and slowly began to lift my right arm to grasp the leather cross strap that ran from my left shoulder across the front of my body and attached to my gun belt. My thought was *if I can just get my arm in front of my heart maybe I'll be able to deflect the blade from a direct hit*. Then, as I began to talk to the man his shakiness began to subside, even as the blade remained pointed directly at my chest, and his story began to unfold.

It seemed he and another man had been joint owners of bar in a prominent local hotel. It was a vibrant business; everything seemed to be going well until one day, to his complete surprise, his wife left him for his trusted partner. Then to compound matters his wife and partner sued him claiming that his half of the business actually belonged to her and not to him. So he stood not only to lose his wife but also his livelihood. All this had taken place within the last couple of years and both parties had attorneys working on the civil action. He said they were very close to a solution that would see him receive a cash settlement, an amount that would at least allow him to leave town and start a new life somewhere else. Then the final straw broke. All of the legal papers supporting his claim had just been lost in a very suspicious fire and his case had folded like a house of cards – he would be left with nothing after all. He was fuming and clearly intent on killing both of them. In fact, he was on his way to do exactly that when he called the police.

For an hour we talked and I tried to convince him that while he believed he had good reason to kill his wife and partner, he really had no justifiable reason to want to kill me. (Self-preservation is indeed an interesting motivator). But I also told him that in truth the very fact that he had called the police, literally on himself, was evidence to me that he was really no killer at all and really crying for help. In due time he broke down in tears, handed me the knife, and we left together to find him some professional assistance. I guess a lot of folks can get pushed to the brink by the actions of others which can sometimes have disastrous side effects.

In the early 1960's times were changing the face of policing. In the United States demonstrations against the Vietnam War and civil rights riots were bringing police officers face to face with violence on a daily basis. And the effects were being felt even as far afield as Canada. In fact I remember one day speaking to a group of about five hundred elementary school students on the topic *Friendship with the Police* when a young boy in grade eight stood up with tears in his eyes and asked,

How can you tell us you're our friend when your brothers in Chicago are beating people with sticks?

It was a tough question to answer. But violence was certainly becoming more prevalent in British Columbia where policing often seemed more akin to the type of policing found in the United States than other parts of Canada, particularly areas like the Maritimes and Prairie Provinces which tended to be much less hostile. In fact prior to the 1960's most police officers in those regions could well expect to serve until they retired to pension without ever having drawn a gun or been involved in any weapon related incidents. But officers in British Columbia began experiencing more and more incidents where life threatening situations were encountered and every indicator was pointing towards its ever increasing nature.

When escaped convicts stole a police car at gun point and were apprehended after a shot gun blast fired from another pursuing police car blew out the taillights of the hijacked cruiser the reality really began to strike home to all of us stationed in Kamloops. More and more often members were faced with incidents where their lives could easily have been forfeited, like the night two officers, Cst. Larry Wagner and Cst. Kelly Kuchta, violated our standing orders of, *one patrolman per vehicle,* and attended together to the early morning complaint of an estranged husband harassing his former wife. As they drove up to the street address they observed an idling vehicle parked in the alley behind the house, and then, as they began to exit the vehicle, the subject appeared from behind a tree and leveled a rifle at Larry. It became a scene frozen in time. Kelly was standing on the driver's side of the police car. Larry was still seated in the vehicle and the gunman was pointing the gun directly at his head, poised to pull the trigger. Later they described the look in the gunman's eyes as they flashed from Larry – to Kelly – to the rifle and back again, as if some strange debate were taking place in his mind then, without warning, he rotated the barrel up under his chin and fired. He fell back on the sidewalk and as they rushed to his aid the strangest thing happened, the woman who had complained, ran from the house and berated them for killing her husband.

Later investigation revealed that the rifle contained only one round of ammunition and, even though the gunman had additional cartridges in his pockets, he could not have reloaded in time to deal with the second officer. Both officers were convinced that had only one of them arrived at the scene they would have surely been killed. The debate in the gunman's mind was obviously how he was going to cope with that second officer if he killed the first. Sadly, even to this day, most police forces still sacrifice officer's lives for economic reasons. I was thankful I wasn't at the scene although I was on the same shift when the incident took place, but it wasn't long before I would also have to tackle a few more dangerous incidents.

One of those episodes took place on a warm summer's night. I was patrolling with an auxiliary member, who is simply, an unarmed civilian volunteer who is provided with a uniform, a minimum of training and simply intended to accompany a regular officer on patrol. An auxiliary could be of great assistance and often helped in overcoming the problems encountered by an officer patrolling alone, but on this occasion one of them almost got himself killed. It started with a call concerning a man holding a group of people at gunpoint in the front yard of a residential home adjacent to the downtown business district. What didn't immediately register was that the location was a known haunt of the city's local motorcycle gang.

As we arrived we could clearly see a man with a rifle holding a group of people at bay in the front yard. As I pulled the police car to a stop near the front yard the rifleman saw us and dashed around the corner of the house. Even while I was still parking the vehicle the auxiliary member leapt from the car in hot pursuit of the subject. They were a block into the commercial business district before I was safely out of the police car. I was more upset with the auxiliary than the rifleman. It's not bravery to chase a man with a gun when you're unarmed – if I could bottle that kind of response I could make a fortune selling it as *instant stupid*.

By the time I reached the business district I could see the rifleman a block and a half ahead with the auxiliary about half a block behind him. Then as the rifleman passed the Hudson's Bay store he made a sharp turn to the right. Since I was on the next adjacent street I decided to cut to the right as well thinking he may well try to cut back to his original area. And that is exactly what he did. When he got to the end of the building he made another turn to the right, I turned left and there we stood face to face about ten yards apart, me with my revolver in my hand, and him with his rifle now held horizontally across the front of his body. We froze in our steps! It was a true Mexican standoff. But then the ridiculous happened, the auxiliary member came stumbling out of an alleyway right between us, came to an exhausted halt, turned his head back toward me and said,

Oh there you are.

My first thought was – *You're a dead man!*

I thought for sure the rifleman would shoot him. I didn't answer – instead I jumped into the doorway of the Hudson's Bay store and aimed my revolver at the gunman. Now with my body ninety percent concealed and only my head, hands and revolver exposed, I called for the subject to throw down his weapon. He evaluated his options. Then, slowly and methodically, his left hand slid down the rifle barrel to the end of the barrel and in a deliberate slow motion he released his right hand from the trigger and the rifle stock, then, he began raising his right hand and lowering the butt of the rifle until he was holding it vertically with only his fingers on the tip of the barrel. Still maintaining eye contact with me, he bent forward and laid the rifle on the sidewalk. A deadly confrontation had been avoided with no thanks to my brainless assistant. Little did I know at the time that one day I would again have intimate dealings with this same individual but on a much more personal level.

For some reason knives have always frightened me even more than guns. Perhaps it some naive belief that it might not hurt as much to be shot as to stabbed, but as strange as it may seem there are also times, probably in the lives of most police officers, when they may not even be aware of a life threatening situation. Such was the case one night in Kamloops, when I was dispatched to investigate a call of possible shots being fired in a field adjacent to a sports complex. There were no vehicles in the area when I arrived and no sign of anyone in the adjoining field. I searched around briefly using my flashlight and then simply returned to my other duties. Then, a few weeks later, another officer told me that during a subsequent investigation he had learned something more of the incident that took place that night. Apparently, I wasn't alone after all. A lone gunman was lying in the tall grass adjacent to the sports field. He held a high powered rifle in his hands, his finger on the trigger and he followed my form around the field all the while pretending to pull the trigger and making whispering rifle sounds, *pssh, pssh, pssh.* I was a trigger pull away from eternity. It was a startling enlightenment that brought on a whole new round of *what ifs*.

29
Dead Babies Don't Cry

When the young Indian boy walked up to the counter in the Kamloops Detachment he had a worried look on his face. He was only fourteen years old, yet his countenance betrayed years of accumulative sadness. When I asked if I could help him his eyes watered and he said,

I think the baby's dead, he doesn't cry and I can't wake him up.

As the story unfolded he told me he had been left to babysit several children as the adults had gone to Kelowna for a weekend retreat. I accompanied him to the small house in the lower part of town and was immediately struck by the unkept nature of the home. Never would I have thought that a baby's crib could be lost in a small bedroom, but such was the accumulation of junk and litter that I actually had to have him lead me to the place where the crib was concealed behind the masses of debris.

The baby was still in the crib, lying on its back and holding its bottle, though the milk within it had now curdled and soured. The child was clearly dead and my heart went out to the young boy who felt so responsible for the tragedy.

As the investigation continued other officers arrived at the scene, the coroner was advised and indicated his intention to attend and I notified the local government welfare agency with a request that they come and remove three remaining children from the premises. It was my intention that they could be better cared for at some other location until the parents returned. In the meantime, the three tiny tots huddled together under a single blanket on a mattress in one of the adjoining bedrooms.

Dr. Smilie, the chief Coroner, arrived and began to conduct his own investigation before allowing for the body to be removed. Meanwhile, police officers snapped pictures and recorded various details to be included in our report. It was then that the woman from the Social Services Agency arrived on the scene. In a condescending manner she asked for me and when I identified myself she wasted no time in telling me just how inconvenient this all was. It was, after all, evening and although she was indeed, *on-call,* she seriously questioned the importance of my request. Then in a caustic voice she asked,

Just what seems to be the problem?

Briefly I relayed to her what had transpired, lead her to the second bedroom and silently indicated the children, now huddled together and pretending to be asleep. Then I said,

It was my hope that you would take these children and keep them until their parents return next week.

Considering her attitude her response was not entirely unexpected,

Well, they're fine now, in fact they are all sleeping. I have no intention of taking them out of here!

The sarcasm in my answer surprised her as I came back with,

Surely you speak in jest, you think those children are asleep with flash bulbs popping and police officers stumbling through every room. I want these children out of here!

Her face narrowed in bitterness and she said,

The police don't tell us how to do our jobs. The children will stay.

Apparently, it was the final straw for Dr. Smilie, who had overheard the entire conversation. He came storming out of the room where the deceased child lay and confronted the social worker. He stood inches from her face and said,

I'm Dr. Smilie, the Coroner, and I am telling you to get those children out of this house now!

My ego was flooded with vindication as she silently blushed and hurriedly made the arrangements necessary to have the children removed to foster care until their parents could return.

I have attended many autopsies in my life, but surely those involving babies and small children are the most difficult to endure. Sometimes a pathologist can ease the suffering of an outside observer by explaining in detail exactly what they are looking for during an autopsy, but police officers often have to attend in order to collect parts of the body, such as portions of the brain, liver and stomach contents, in order to have them further examined in a forensic laboratory. Now, in the dissection of an adult one can concentrate on a single portion of the body and sometimes fool yourself into believing that it is just the butchering of a piece of meat, but with a small child, the whole body is visible during the entire procedure, and nothing can rectify or camouflage its true nature. Fortunately for me I only had to endure two such autopsies in my career. This was my first.

The second occurred simply because I answered the detachment telephone as the man on the other end, in a shaky voice said, *I just found a baby in a garbage can.* I attended with Cst. Dennis Smith and at the scene we found two city sanitation workers sitting morbidly near the rear of a garbage truck in an alley in downtown Kamloops. In the back of the truck, thrown in with the putrid garbage, was a white sweater and wrapped inside the body of a small new born baby.

Dennis lead the investigation and we began with a search of nearby hotels. Our break came the second day when we spotted what looked like splatters of blood beneath the toilet bowl in the woman's washroom of a local hotel. When we questioned hotel staff about it the clerk's response was telling,

You should have seen it the day before yesterday, there was blood everywhere.

When we inquired if anyone working at the hotel was pregnant we were told that only one person was and she had phoned in sick. They also told us that this young lady had been denying for months that she actually was pregnant. We surmised that we were getting closer to an answer.

When we arrived at Beverly's house Dennis lead the way as we ascended the steps to the front door. The steps were at an angle to the house and were adjacent to a window that looked into the kitchen. As we climbed the stairs we looked into the window and saw two women, one younger, one older, sitting at the kitchen table. With one glance at their faces, Dennis turned back to me and said,

We've got the right place.

Beverly's mother invited us in without the slightest hesitation and when we looked at Beverly we could see a pool of fluid on the floor beneath her chair and fluid still periodically dripping from her body. In the short conversation that followed she vehemently denied having had a child but willingly agreed to attend with us at the Royal Alexandria Hospital for a physical examination. The doctor confirmed that she had given birth within the last twenty-four hours. Beverly told him he was a liar.

Forensic investigation later confirmed Beverly's hand prints above the toilet in the hotel washroom and marks on the wall where it was believed she had struck the baby against the wall. The white sweater, although it contained no markings or tags did contain hair consistent with Beverly and notwithstanding that her mother had thoroughly washed all of her clothing, forensic examination found the infant's blood still adhering to the fibers. Her mother solidly supported her denial. But psychiatric evidence indicated that Beverly, who already had a previous child out of wedlock, was so distraught about another pregnancy, that she had completely blocked it out of her mind. To Beverly she simply *was not pregnant*.

A Governor General's Warrant committed her to a mental hospital until she would come to grips with the truth of her sad mental state.

30

Trouble at the Silver Grill

There's one in every city – a Chinese restaurant that caters to the late-night crowd. In Revelstoke it was the WK Café where fights were commonplace and officers would regularly answer the detachment telephone only to hear the frantic caller cry out, *WK Café - evey - ting bwoken up here - come qwik!,* then hang up with no further clarification, generally, none was needed.

The city of Kamloops was no exception; its contribution was the *Silver Grill Cafe.* Not an entirely bad place by its own standards, but one again that remained open late into the night and thereby attracted some fairly savory characters and few weekend midnight shifts would pass without at least one call from the Silver Grill.

It was early March in 1969 when Corporal Danielson's skeleton crew of just four officers and one auxiliary member were left to police the entire city. It was the night of the Annual Police Ball and the shift's three additional members were given special leave to attend the celebration. A move that didn't sit well with the remaining officers who knew they would be run off their feet responding to the usual influx of calls during another weekend midnight shift. And since one officer had to remain in the office to answer the telephone and perform dispatch duties only three were available to complete the standard property checks and respond to requests for police attendance.

Since numerous business properties had to be individually patrolled and personally checked Corporal Danielson asked each member to patrol alone in different areas. The Corporal and I would split the North Kamloops region and Cst. Shaw accompanied by an auxiliary member would respond to complaints on the south side of the river in the downtown core. Once the numerous north shore properties had been checked we would reunite on the south side and join the effort there. It was a hectic schedule but worked well, until the call from the Silver Grill Café.

From the radio calls I overheard it appeared that a dispute had arisen between two patrons in the café and in anger someone had threatened to throw a pot of hot coffee in their opponent's face. Constable Shaw and his accompanying auxiliary member were dispatched to attend and Danielson and I began making our way back towards the south side of the city as back up. Of course, by the time the investigating officers arrived at the Silver Grill the combatant had left the premises and the situation had seemingly resolved itself. Then returning to their police car the officers began a casual search of the surrounding area and as they turned into the alley immediately behind the cafe they saw a man, matching the description of the offending participant, walking down the lane way. Constable Shaw exited the police car and walked after the man calling out for him to stop. Then he saw his quarry make a hunching movement with his shoulders and heard the clicking sounds of automatic pistol being cocked. Then, even as Shaw drew his own weapon, the man spun around. Both men now stood face to face, twenty feet apart, guns leveled. Shaw's unarmed auxiliary partner, who had remained in the police car, was instantly on the radio requesting assistance and I heard him say,

We need help - the guy has a gun on Doug.

There was an eerie pause and at that very moment Corporal Danielson and I were simultaneously crossing the Overland Bridge in an accelerated race to the scene. Danielson told me to approach from the opposite direction anticipating that we could thereby trap the suspect between us. Then the radio cracked to life again and its message was chilling,

They're shooting it out!

The sounds of the gunfire could be heard in the background even as the message was being delivered. My heart was in my throat and my own gun was in my hand and I leaned far over to the right passenger side of the police car and slowly turned into the opposite end of alley where the incident was taking place. I could see the headlights of Shaw's police car directly ahead of me and there was Doug, revolver in hand, leaning against one of the concrete pillars that studded the construction site of an intended parkade, but the suspect was no where to be seen. Unexpectedly, the radio blurted out another message,

He's heading towards the train yards.

The station and its adjacent rail yards were located directly across the next street immediately to the North and I knew that if our culprit reached it our chances of finding him would be next to nil. Leaving my car I retreated to the adjacent street and ran toward the station.

Now sometimes in the midst of a crisis something truly *funny* can happen and at that moment it did. A fellow, who was obviously a trainman on his way home after his shift, was crossing the street, swinging his lunch bucket from side to side and whistling a light-hearted tune. Suddenly, he caught a glimpse of me running directly towards him - gun in hand. As I waved my gun at him and hollered for him to get out of the way his whistle became one of those dry-throated imitations that reminded me of my own feeble first attempt to produce that much coveted sound. He stumbled, stammered and quickly departed from the scene, but I somehow couldn't help but chuckle just a little even there in the middle of a time of truly intensified emotional stress.

As I turned back towards the scene there was still no sign of the suspect and I knew he must still be somewhere in the construction site. Quickly I ran to the corner of the adjacent building and carefully peaked around the corner. Then I saw him. He was hiding behind a large concrete slab, probably the foundation walls for a future elevator. In the distance I could also see Shaw still standing in his original position.

The parking lot of the building where I stood bordered the construction zone and although the parking lot itself was open to the street the remainder of the area was blocked by a thin plywood barrier erected to separate the neighboring sidewalk from the messy work site. Only the parking lot could afford the suspect an unobstructed escape route to the train yard although it was still possible that he could jump the waist high plywood fencing. Still I realized that I had to get to the fenced area if I intended to seriously block his attempt to escape.

I made an instant decision and dashed into the open parking lot to make for the fence. It was a mistake. At the same moment my assailant fired again in Doug's direction, turned and ran into the same open space. Time stood still. We both froze there in the middle of no man's land. Then, both guns blazed – bullets whizzed by, and my mind asked my body – *Are you hit?* Strangely, my thoughts reminded me of rumors I had heard of those who were shot but never realized it until moments later. My eyes seemed to quickly survey the storm coat I wore for the presence of bullet holes. He fired three times, I fired twice. He jumped back behind his concrete sanctuary and I suddenly found myself crouched behind the plywood which had been my hopeful destination. Apparently, neither of us was an expert marksman, but then again moving targets and pounding hearts don't make for much precision.

Suddenly Corporal Danielson appeared at my side not ten feet to my right – having come from the other direction. His plan had worked to perfection. Both of us now had the gunman in sight from behind the veil of our paper thin plywood shield. Regardless, I was greatly relieved at his presence particularly because I also knew that Dan was one of the finest marksmen in the entire province. I turned to Dan and asked,

Should we shoot him?

He replied,

Not yet – I'll aim high, you aim low, and we'll try to talk him out.

I don't recall exactly what Dan said but I will never forget our assailants reply as he shouted back,

F..... .... I have six left come and get em!

With that he turned, raised his gun towards Doug and I fired. My bullet struck him in the thigh and spun him around – we saw the gun fly from his hand, we jumped the fence and sprinted to get to him before he could retrieve it. As we dragged him screaming to the police car and conveyed him to the hospital he continued his verbal barrage and promised he'd kill me.

It has never ceased to amaze me how completely calm a person can be in the face of such danger. I was thankful that I didn't fold – that I didn't cut and run – my reasoning had been clear – my instincts and actions decisive – my hands steady as a rock – yet just moments afterward I fell apart. My mouth was dry, my hands shook, my heart sank and the usual symptoms of shock came crashing down upon me; and those dastardly *what ifs* again flooded my mind.

The court determined we would have been justified to kill the accused and I knew in my own mind that had I killed him in our first heated exchange of gunfire I would have been fully justified, but I also had no reservations about only wounding him in our final confrontation. I just felt differently at that particular moment. It was like I was more in control of the situation and I was clearly not in as much fear for my own life as I had originally been. I suppose only those who have been there can understand such minute differences. Anyway, I have never even been a hunter – I just couldn't handle taking the life of even an innocent animal – always figured it would be more of a *sport* if the animal also had a gun, but of course, there'd probably be a lot of dead hunters. Maybe it harkens back to my teen years when during my first hunting expedition with my brother-in-law I watch a wounded rabbit sitting on its haunches wiping tears from his eyes with both paws as my brother-in-law finished the job and dispatched the poor thing. Me, I would have taken him to the nearest vet. It was my first and last hunt.

In any event both the courts and the RCMP called us heroes and I was awarded a very nice letter of commendation that read,

COMMANDING OFFICER'S COMMENDATION

I am pleased to commend Constable Robert Arthur Dolman for the courage and restraint he exercised in the events which occurred in the early morning hours of March 8, 1969, at Kamloops, B.C. during the arrest of an armed and dangerous man who had fired at members of the Force.

Constable Dolman's fortitude has brought credit to himself and the Force.

(Signed) G.R. Engel
Assistant Commissioner
Commanding "E" Division
Victoria, B.C.
28 May 69

Yet, I never considered myself a hero, and you'll notice that many of the so called *heroes* you sometimes see interviewed on the evening news often reflect a similar attitude. They don't see themselves as heroes at all; just people doing what had to be done at a particular moment in time. Perhaps that's why someone once described a hero as *just someone who hangs in there for one more minute.* And I think that about sums it up, all of us that night just hung in for one more minute.

At that time the RCMP had no internal support mechanism to offer its members and after this rather disturbing incident those involved were simply expected to *suck it up* and get back to work. Today, while people more fully grasp how such incidents impact one's psyche few still really seem to fully comprehend how post traumatic stress can become a lifetime companion. Even today, when counseling systems are in place, I still seriously doubt that anyone can offer satisfactory consolation to those affected by such trauma, particularly advisors who have never been exposed to such incidents themselves. Theory is one thing, practice is quite another.

Coincidentally, I happened to read recently of a man who drove by an accident scene and successfully leveled a law suit against the government for exposing him to such trauma on the highway. He could no longer work and sadly he received a major monetary settlement. Notwithstanding, of course, how seriously such a decision should be questioned, I couldn't help but wonder how any country could ever begin to reimburse its servicemen, police officers, paramedics, doctors, nurses, or firefighters whose exposure to such incidents and circumstances have left them with the inevitable psychological scars. Here was a man who merely *drove by* an accident scene. But what of those who handled the bodies and dealt personally with the gory details? Surely such a decision disrespects those who really do the *dirty work* in our society.

In any event, the perpetrator in our case was sentenced to seven years in prison for attempted murder and I wish I could say that the episode ended there, but sadly, it did not. Since our friend was the member of a local motorcycle gang death threats continued to circulate and the people making those threats were quite capable of carrying them out. For months I lived with the realization that at any vulnerable moment I could be confronted by those intent on retaliating for what they saw as an assault against one of the own. I was continually armed, carrying a gun even when *off duty*. As far as the Force was concerned nothing had changed and subsequently when *on duty* I was still required to patrol alone. Midnight shifts were the most disconcerting but the coolness of the spring nights allowed me to wear my storm coat and carry my gun in my pocket as I performed my required property checks in back alleys and around darkened buildings.

My nerves were clearly becoming frayed. The slightest unexpected noise would only increase my anxiety. Then, one night, about three o'clock in the morning, I left my patrol car to check the back doors of the businesses in a local shopping center in North Kamloops. As usual my right hand clasped the butt of my service revolver even as my left hand rattled doorknobs. Then, as I approached the shadows of a deeply recessed doorway, a figure lunged forward, screamed and charged directly towards me. I drew my revolver but did not fire and the figure flew by me. I pocketed my weapon, ran after the fleeing form, reached out and grabbed the back of its coat. We both came to a sudden stop and I found myself face to face with a mentally deranged young woman. I remember closing my eyes and thinking to myself, *Oh, my God, I might have killed her.*

Clearly something had to be done. I was either going to have a mental breakdown or even worse make a wrong decision some night that I would regret for the rest of my life. The girl in the alley was a warning, perhaps even a foreshadowing, of what might come to pass if the situation wasn't reconciled. I had to do something.

I respected Corporal Dan Danielson, my squad leader. He was there the night of the shooting, he knew about the threats being made towards me and he was a man I could truly trust. So I went to Dan, asked him if he would help me resolve the situation and we both agreed that only a direct approach would work. I had to confront those making the threats. He would go with me, but he told me that it was only me that could deal with it. For the first time in my career policing was no longer the objective enforcement of the law. The RCMP, the courts, and the entire justice system were oblivious to my problem and now it had become personal. It was just *me* against *them*. What bothered me, however, was that the man behind the threats was also the man I had confronted with a rifle in front of the Hudson's Bay store a year earlier. He was now the leader of the motorcycle gang and wasn't to be taken lightly. But my decision was made, it was now or never.

Dan and I left the office together and patrolled the city in an unsuccessful search for our target. Then, just as we were about to give up for the night, a fellow officer told us he had just seen our target near the local train station, in fact, hardly a stones throw from where the original incident had taken place. When we arrived we approached a group of well-known individuals and I asked their leader if I might speak to him in private. He agreed and we walked to a more isolated location in a nearby park.

I'm not a brave man. Inwardly I was frightened and nervous, though apparently it wasn't obvious to my companion. I wanted desperately to turn and run away. I felt I had been left alone to face this threat. If the Force didn't care anymore than that for me, why should I care about any of this? I had a wife and family to worry about. It was an interesting but one-sided conversation and I began by asking,

Do you know who I am?

He replied, *Sure.*

My response came boiling out,

Well, I hear you and your friends want to kill me and I just want you to know that although I could have killed your buddy I didn't, but I will tell you this – this is no longer about you and the police – its become personal – I don't like the threats I'm hearing and I want you to tell anyone interested in coming after me that I've reloaded my gun and I will kill the next son of .... that comes after me.

Donny didn't reply he only stared. Strangely, he never seemed to fit the mold of those he associated with and inwardly I had a weird respect for him. Perhaps deep down inside I could see visions of myself if time and chance had fashioned my life differently. We weren't really that much different Donny and I. But he understood that this was no idle threat and indeed it was not meant to be. For me it had come down to the personal and as much as I regret it had to come to that I was thankful that I had at least confronted the issue. Now at least both sides knew what the stakes were. Within weeks the threats waned and in a few months my life returned to normal and my revolver back to the holster where it belonged.

31
The Whole Truth

Daily exposure to the harsh realities of everything from broken homes to broken bodies can drain the marrow from one's life and leave a person cold and bitter. As a matter of fact, although many would likely never admit it, at some point in their first few years of service every police officer must come to recognize the boundaries and limitations of their duties, resolving to present to the courts the reasonable and the probable grounds upon which they base their accusations and leave final judgment within the jurisdiction of the legal system, or by default they will choose to take these issues personally, resenting poor decisions and becoming hardened and bitter when they see the guilty scoff and victims suffer. Whether this decision is made consciously or subconsciously is a moot point, but their choice is easily discernible and often reflected in their personality.

I resolved very early in my career to *tell it like it is,* and when testifying in court, *to tell the truth, the whole truth and nothing but the truth, so help me God.* I was to learn very quickly, however, that one does not need to lie in order to shade the meaning of their testimony. In fact one really only needs not to tell the *whole truth* – half of the truth can sometimes be as damaging as an outright lie. Of course, there is one thing about telling the truth of which you may be absolutely certain – *Truth doesn't change with time*. Trials can easily drag on for months or even years and witnesses who fudge the truth during their initial examination struggle to recall their previous answers in subsequent trials. The truth is always the simplest thing to remember. But what happens when the prosecuting attorney doesn't really want the *whole truth*?

One night in Kamloops, B.C. I arrested a young man lying under a semi-trailer truck near a building which had just been broken into. My investigation clearly showed that he was indeed the culprit. But when I brought him back to the police station and began to book him on the charges I found him to be incoherent and completely out of touch with the reality of the moment. So after I had escorted him to his jail cell I paid a visit to my shift commander, Sgt. Ozzie Zorn to inform him of my findings. I explained to him that this young man could not possibly have formed the *intent* to be held criminally responsible for what he had done. Zorn replied with a question,

Do you have reasonable and probable grounds to believe that he committed this crime?

I said, *Absolutely!*

And then he said this,

Then it's your job to take that information before the court – you are not the court – you just tell the truth and the court will decide whether or not the accused could form the intent to commit the crime.

He was right, my job was to investigate and present the evidence. I was neither the judge nor the jury.

Several months later the trial was held and I testified concerning the evidence I found that gave me reason to believe the accused had committed the offence. The prosecutor seemed pleased and everything was perfectly aligned to ensure a conviction. But then the defence lawyer asked me for my opinion on the personal condition of the accused at the time of his arrest. I said,

Well, I'm not a psychiatrist or a physician but if you want my personal opinion, I would say the accused was mentally confused.

The defence lawyer was delighted. The judge was shocked. Here was the arresting officer, a witness for the prosecution, giving evidence that would undoubtedly lead to a dismissal. Following a little further clarification, the judge dismissed the case and declared the accused *not guilty*. Clearly, justice had been served; the accused had committed the offence, but the court had decided, based on the *whole truth* that he could not possibly have formed the *intent* necessary to be held legally responsible. It was exactly how the system was supposed to work.

But when I stepped down from the witness stand and walked past the prosecuting attorney he turned to me and in a rude and insulting manner said,

Boy, you sure blew that didn't you?

I was instantly infuriated, turned to him, and shot back,

Well, maybe this is a good example of a person that shouldn't be convicted.

The judge smiled.

But this wouldn't be the only time I would butt heads with prosecutor attorneys in their pursuit of the *whole truth*. On another occasion I testified as a witness for the prosecution during the trial of a young man who had been charged with leaving the scene of an accident, impaired driving and attempting to escape lawful custody. He was convicted on all counts. But before the trial concluded the defence attorney, because I was personally familiar with this young man, asked if I would appear as a *character witness* on his behalf before he was sentenced. I agreed.

Testifying as a *character witness* is an entirely different type of testimony and much more leeway is afforded to the witnesses to give personal opinions. So the judge asked me what I knew of this young man and whether or not what had taken place was out of character for him. So I told him that I did know him, that he played hockey for the local junior hockey team, and that this incident was indeed out of character for him. Then the judge asked how I might then explain what took place. So I said,

Well, your honour I think I know exactly what happened. He was crossing the Overlander Bridge when he sideswiped a vehicle heading in the opposite direction. At the same time he saw a police car directly behind him. He had been drinking and he knew he was in trouble. So he did not stop – thus the failing to stop at an accident charge. When the police finally pulled him over, they found he had been drinking, arrested him for impaired driving and put him in the back of the police car. Then, he simply panicked, climbed out of the cruiser and tried to run away – thus the charge of attempting to escape custody. I know this young man, he's not at all like that. I believe he made a stupid mistake and I don't believe it will ever happen again.

Now of course, he had already been convicted of the offences, but the judge clearly took my testimony into account, the sentencing was light and the young man was able to continue with his hockey career. Was justice served? Absolutely, and as for me, I wasn't really just trying to be a nice guy; I was simply telling the *whole truth*.

And I believe it was that kind of testimony that caused the same judge to summon me to his chambers when he heard I was transferred from Kamloops, where he thanked me for the nature of my testimony during my years of service in that city. I had never heard of such a thing happening before and I must sadly admit I have never heard of it again since. Later in my career as an expert in the RCMP's Forensic Laboratory I would testify on hundreds of occasions on every type of case from fraud to murder, but I never wavered from that one simple rule that was restated to me every time I took the witness stand,

Do you swear to tell the truth, the whole truth and nothing but the truth, so help you God.

Strange how simply telling the truth works.

32
The Last Straw

I suppose the final straw came through a man named John Booth. As I mentioned in an earlier chapter three RCMP officers were killed in Kamloops in 1962 by a man named George Booth, who had subsequently been killed by other officers following a short man hunt. George's father, John, who was somewhat mentally fragile, never accepted the RCMP version of the events that took place that day and consequently held the police unreservedly responsible for his son's death.

John lived as a recluse in a rustic cabin in the hills not far from the RCMP Sub-Division which was located on the Trans-Canada Highway and since his home was not far from where his son had been killed he proceeded to build a memorial at the site. Sadly, a few of the local youths would occasionally vandalize it and draw unwittingly close to instigating a showdown between John and the police, whom he held responsible for such attacks.

Publicly, John made no secret of the fact that he intended to kill more police officers before he died than his son had and since he was mentally unstable, usually carried a weapon and was known to have a short fuse, local officers considered it best to leave him well enough alone. So when John would stagger down the street in a drunken stupor crying out, *Ding, ding, ding, I'm the captain of the ship*, he was intentionally ignored. Superior officers knew full well that arresting John for some minor violation could be the spark that ignited a confrontation that was bound to end badly for all concerned. It was a sound advice to keep John Booth at arms length and hope that his advancing age might allow him to die peacefully. But so serious were John's threats that no one doubted that, if John lived long enough, he would one day come down the mountainside and seek his revenge on those he held responsible for his son's death. He even painted his rifle sights white so he could more clearly align targets in the dark and at the nearby Sub-division Headquarters, window blinds were ordered closed day and night as a preventative measure. John Booth was a truly dangerous man.

Every new member posted to the Kamloops RCMP was required to know who John Booth was, to recognize him on sight, to not only be familiar with the history of the Booth tragedy, but also realize the potential danger and act accordingly. I knew John Booth just as well as anyone in the detachment and yet even then when the day came for my confrontation with him I failed to immediately grasp who it was that I was dealing with.

There were several reasons for my ignorance that day when John presented himself at the front desk of the Kamloops City Detachment. For one thing, I had just returned from a three month course at the Forensic Laboratory in Regina and my mind was still a thousand miles away. The second was the birth of our daughter Tanis on the 8th of June, 1971. Our family was now four and we were thankful to have exactly the family we desired. In any event my mind was elsewhere as our five o'clock shift began and ten or twelve officers milled about conversing with one another. That's when a man *dressed in a suit*, which incidentally, John Booth never wore, walked through the front door. Thinking him to be someone requesting assistance I casually approached the counter and asked if I could help him. Suddenly I realized who it was – it was John Booth and his opening statement almost made my knees buckle, he said,

Today's the day – I've come down.

Then, it dawned on me – it that was June 18th – the anniversary of his son's murder of the three RCMP officers and his subsequent death. At that moment I truly believed I was about to die.

There is an old adage that says *familiarity breeds contempt* and in police work it stands as a solid truth. Officers often die needlessly because they fall into the habit of thinking the routine and familiar will never foster danger. After walking up to hundreds of vehicles to ask the driver to produce a driver's license or attending to yet another fruitless family fight officers often become careless and thereby sometimes seemingly contribute to their own death. It happens over and over again and I immediately felt like I was about to be the latest example of such stupidity.

If there was no other reason that I should have been more aware it was that anniversary dates are highly significant to people like John who are trying to make some personal statement but the long familiarity of those dates uneventfully passing caused all of us to be completely ignorant of the significance of the 18th of June. I knew then why John Booth was dressed in his finest and probably his only suit. And it was the perfect scenario, with so many members milling about and socializing during a shift change he now had the opportunity he had long hoped for – to kill more members than his son had. For John the setting could not have been more ideal, except for one thing, he surely never expected to run into someone as stupid as me and I feigned complete ignorance of the significance of his statement and said,

I'm sorry sir; I don't quite understand what you're saying.

He became angry and irritated. He had obviously prided himself in the knowledge that every police officer knew him, but now he was confronted by someone who didn't and he needed to explain himself. I believe to this day that he would no doubt have enjoyed killing someone who had recognized him, but it was becoming clear that he wouldn't get the same satisfaction by killing an idiot like me. For my part, I was doing my best to stall for time hoping that at least someone else would recognize who it was standing across the counter. Then, as if wanting to further enlighten me he asked,

Don't you know who I am?

I said,

No sir, I'm afraid I don't.

And he replied,

I'm the one what they killed my boy – Today's the day – and I've come down.

When I still appeared confused he began to explain to me what had happened, how the police had killed his son in the hills and how he had vowed that one day he would come down from the hills and take more with him when he died than his son had. I just listened but the thought ran through my mind how sad it was to have this old man's story the last thing I ever heard.

Somehow my continued ignorance seemed to strike some soft spot in old John because since I could no longer claim ignorance of the events he seemed to soften a little and he said,

I know that some of you guys are alright, but you know, it was the bad ones what killed my boy, you know that don't you son?

I reluctantly agreed,

I know that sir.

Then he said,

And you know that one day I got to come down for them, don't you son?

I nodded,

Yes, sir I know that.

174

Although I dearly wanted to add,

But just not today John!

It was at that moment that Cst. Kuchta recognized John, separated himself from the group and was keeping a watchful eye on the conversation. With his awareness and John's apparent softening the situation had at least cooled. Then old John said,

Okay son, then I'll go now.

He turned and walked out of the station.

I was a basket case for the rest of my shift. There is another saying in some police circles – *dead is dumb,* because so many times officers do something dumb that leads to their own death. In a whole career one mistake is all that's needed. I had made a serious mistake not recognizing John Booth. And at that moment I hoped more than ever that I would get accepted into the forensic laboratory and not have to deal any longer with the John Booths of this world. Within three months my transfer to the Forensic Laboratory in Ottawa came through and I was delighted maybe John Booth had been the last straw after all.

33
Helmets and Horses

If I thought the marble game we learned and enjoyed with friends in Revelstoke was a good diversion from the anxieties of police work, coaching football and horseback riding became my lifetime diversions. I was afraid of horses when I joined the RCMP, but learned to respect and appreciate them during recruit training. And although I never completely trusted any horse and never really considered myself a cowboy or highly qualified rider I still enjoyed hundreds of hours riding with old friends.

I owned only three horses in my twenty years of riding and each had its own distinct personality, but none as much as *Dusty* the young appaloosa mare I bought from a retired RCMP officer. John Dowsett had raised *Dusty* from a colt and she was more like his dog than his horse. Every day neighbours would see him walking along the roadway near his acreage with his arm around her neck as she accompanied him to his mailbox. She followed John everywhere and since John never believed in *breaking* a horse she was tenderly guided into obedience through trust and kindness until one day he simply saddled her up and rode around the yard. She trusted John and he loved her, but John was getting too old to deal with horses anymore and since he could no longer ride he agreed to sell Dusty to me.

Dusty was a delight and her mind seemed always to be in high gear. She was like one of those horses you'd see in the movies or entertaining at county fairs who would use her teeth to pull the blanket off her back when you turned away to pick up the saddle, or toss your spurs over the fence into the garden. She was amazingly curious and one day as we strolled along a highway ditch she decided to examine a large cardboard box lying in the tall grass and then after smelling it and pushing it along on the ground for a few feet she picked it up with her teeth and casually continued on her way playfully swinging it from side to side. Needless to say the passing motorists were quite amused.

But while horseback riding was a welcome respite from the seriousness of the work that surrounded me, coaching football became a practical therapy that blessed with me with an abundance of lifetime friendships and positive memories. I had started coaching football in Regina when I was just seventeen years old and although not every city in which I was stationed had a football program, whenever they did I quickly volunteered. The result was more than twenty-five years coaching in four different provinces and at every level from Atoms at age six to the Junior programs with age limits of twenty two years. I was even fortunate enough to be invited by the Edmonton Eskimos of the Canadian Football League to coach with them during the leagues' 1988 All-star game.

I have always been a fiercely competitive individual, as my wife can attest to during our admittedly infrequent Scrabble contests, and that spirited – never say die, work ethic drove me to develop programs that reflected a high degree of success. My motto always reflected a simple philosophy – *give me a team with heart and I'll beat anybody*, and *once a member of the team you were always a member of the team.*

But it wasn't really me. You see I have always believed that to be successful in any field one should seek to surround themselves with highly qualified people and I have always tried to do that. I was never afraid to bring someone onto my coaching staff who knew more about a particular area than I did. In fact in my experience I think that may well be the reason so many programs fail – the egos of many head coaches prevent them from acquiring assistants who are smarter than they are. The insecurity of coaches even at minor levels is truly astounding. But I realized early in my coaching career that there is no limit to what can be accomplished if no one cares who gets the credit.

Interestingly, during those years I coached a veritable barnyard including Tigers, Lions, Colts, Rams, and Wildcats but there were also Crescents, Reds, Crusaders, Sabres and Eskimos, every one of them special in their own right, all contributing to a wealth of friendships influencing my life and touching the very depths of my soul. They fashioned my life in more ways than they will ever know. Those graduating players are represented in every walk of life, many have become parents, and some have even become football coaches themselves. And still today, in those quiet moments, I can see with my mind's eye the pranks, laughter, elation and the tears we shared together when they strapped on their equipment as boys and took a giant step towards manhood. When we collectively won more than one hundred and thirty games, ten Divisional Titles and nine League Championships. Not surprisingly, football provided me with life-long friendships, a deep abiding love for the game and a common ground of fellowship with my son, Bret, who played and excelled at every level.

The moments I shared with those who associated with me in these pastimes will last forever and the fond memories I have of my association with *helmets* and *horses* I can never forget nor ever hope to repeat.

34
Political Interference

Before my arrival in Ottawa my experience providing security for politicians and dignitaries had been limited. I did escort the Archbishop of Canterbury, Michael Ramsay, across the Roger's Pass in the late sixties and had the privilege of having coffee with him at the Northlander Motor Hotel at the summit of the Roger's Pass. But it was a duty, save for those few minutes of enlightened conversation when he showed me the ring presented to him by the Pope, that passed accompanied only by long periods of boredom, like those spent huddled in the kitchen of a local restaurant, while he was being honored at a lengthy official dinner.

But one political occasion stands out foremost in my mind and that was an incident with Queen Elizabeth in the early seventies in Kamloops, B.C. I was assigned to crowd control duties – simply expected to face the crowd and watch for the unexpected as the Royals walked along the roadway of the Kamloops airport. Prince Philip was on the other side, the Queen walked down the center, and Princess Margaret walked on my side of the roadway. Suddenly, from the corner of my eye I saw a man bolt from the crowd about fifty feet from me and run directly towards the Queen. My basic instincts kicked in and I turned and ran in hot pursuit. Unfortunately, I was not close enough to intercept him and I can still see the shocked look on the Queen's face as he took up a position directly in front of her, reached into his coat to pull something out, and I heard him say,

This is for you!

By that time I was airborne and I saw the Queen's mouth drop open in response to his unexpected statement as my impact drove us both to the ground at her feet. Suddenly, the useless entourage of senior officers that had been following about twenty feet behind her Majesty came scurrying to my assistance and the man was whisked from her presence.

He was escorted to the police station where he was held until the Queen left the city. Interviewing him we soon discovered he was nothing more than a member of the religious Baha'i sect - his offering – simply a Baha'i cross. I was thankful that he wasn't a nut with a gun or a knife; if he had been Queen Elizabeth would have died that day on the asphalt of the Kamloops airport – so much for guaranteeing anyone's personal security. Still I couldn't help but wonder, as I searched a bridge in the middle of night in the back woods of southern Ontario and waited there until her train passed over, if she had any idea the man guarding that lonely bridge was the same one who tackled her cross bearing assailant so many years before in Kamloops – but then how could she?

So I hadn't given much thought to politics and personal security details when I transferred to Ottawa to assume my new position as an understudy in the Document Section of the Forensic Laboratory, but when my instructor, Inspector John Hodgins, placed a flashlight and a snub nose revolver on my desk I knew it was a bad omen. The visits of President Tito of Yugoslavia, Kosygin of Russia and Richard Nixon and once again Queen Elizabeth, were also supplemented by political protests in opposition to a number of controversial events that took place during that time and the constant specter of the radical

FLQ, the Front de libération du Québec, that sought Quebec independence.

Since Ottawa is the location of Canada's central government it is often the focal point of political protest, but few Canadians probably realize that common groups of agitators regularly infiltrate the legitimate groups who are there simply to exercise their freedom of expression. For example, when farmers protested on Parliament Hill the Red Maoist organization mingled into their ranks provoking a resulting confrontation with the police officers who manned the crowd control barriers that restricted the movement of the protestors. Sadly, many Canadians don't grasp the fact that, even today, there are elements in our society who support the overthrow of our democratic form of government and who are quick to swell the ranks of any legitimate protest group.

When the Americans proposed to detonate a nuclear weapons test on November 6, 1971 beneath Amchitka Island, in Alaska, my partner and I spent that day watching demonstrators' burn effigies of Richard Nixon and make threatening gestures towards the U.S. Marines guarding the American Consulate, located directly across the street from Parliament Hill. The blast took place at 5:00PM Ottawa time and we anxiously listened as the Peace Tower declared the ominous zero hour.

The protestors had been allowed their hours of freedom, but minutes after the clock stuck five the crowd was quietly ushered onto sidewalks by the Ottawa City Police riot squad, even as city fire trucks dowsed the flames of their bonfires and street sweepers rolled in to clear the debris and allow normal traffic to again flow unhindered down the busy street bordering Parliament Hill. Having seen them in action, I suspect the Ottawa City Police represent some the most highly experienced units in the world when it comes to dealing with such situations. The sheer number of demonstrations in their city probably demands it. Even so I was truly impressed.

In October 1971 the demonstration of 10,000 Jews during Russian Premier Alexei Kosygin's visit to Ottawa labeled me for midnight patrol in the park adjacent to the Russian Embassy. It was an interesting night that saw my partner and I assemble onto picnic tables, the collection of more than eighty Molotov cocktails that we found in the surrounding bushes. Obviously they had been planted there in order to make them readily accessible to at least some of the expected demonstrators.

Other team members patrolling the same neighborhood faced another unusual situation. They observed a suspicious man in a long trench coat walking down the street near the Embassy. Stopping to speak to him they noticed that he kept his hands behind his back during the conversation. When they asked what he was hiding behind his back he simply said, *A bomb,* and handed them the device. And it surely was – dynamite sticks, wire, and a clock. When I saw it a chill ran up my spine.

Morning light saw the two of us replaced by ninety-nine fellow RCMP officers. I remember the number well because my partner Guy and I sat on one of our picnic benches, surrounded by Molotov cocktails, and counted the corporals and sergeants from the headquarters building as they marched into the park in a column of twos. Our catcalls of,

It sure takes a lot of corporals and sergeants to replace two constables,

falling on deaf ears.

It was truly a strange night and although we expected to go home to bed we were instead assigned to a patrol car for the remainder of the day. In those days there was no overtime pay in the RCMP and senior officers often took unfair advantage of that fact and assigned members to long hours and irregular shifts with impunity. My highway patrol duties had often necessitated my working long hours and when I was the only officer qualified to conduct breathalyzer tests on impaired drivers in the city of Kamloops I conducted more than three hundred such tests, most of course, during the wee small hours of the morning, without compensation. In fact, the situation became so ridiculous, that I was not even permitted to report for duty an hour or two late – even when working day shift and after having been called out three times during the previous night. It seemed so much easier for senior offices to refuse any such requests than to make any shift adjustment that might be necessary. It was just the way it was – members followed orders and accepted overtime as part of their required *duty*. In any event by mid-morning of what was now our second shift, the Russian Embassy was surrounded by more than seven hundred police officers, most of them from the Ontario Provincial Police and the RCMP. It was truly a sight to behold.

The Ontario Provincial Police were also a force I respected. They were well trained and well organized and I was never more impressed than when their *cafeteria bus* rolled into the parking lot near the embassy. No, I'm not kidding; they actually had a bus that catered meals on-site to their members. Hot dogs, hamburgers, fries and sandwiches were in abundance. Our mouths were watering as we watched them belly up to their mobile convenience store, which unfortunately for us was only available to their own members. But of course the RCMP had different ideas, and only after someone finally realized that their members might also have to eat, did they finally order *box lunches* sent over from Divisional Headquarters. Thankfully, they had forgotten to prepare one for Guy and I since more than half of the ninety-nine members they served that day suffered food poisoning. I'm sure most would much more have preferred the cholesterol consumption available to the OPP.

Luckily, we were at the Russian Embassy and not assigned to Parliament Hill where an even larger gathering of officers had been provided to protect Prime Minister Trudeau and Soviet Premier Alexei Kosygin, because that was the day Trudeau, decided to alter the prescribed route and walk to their next appointment. It was a mistake that might have cost Kosygin his life when a man sprung from the crowd and onto his back shouting, *"Free Hungary!"* And although Kosygin was not injured the embarrassment to the Canadian government was considerable. Of course the blame was quickly diverted from the Prime Minister to the RCMP and more than a hundred police officers were required to provide written statements explaining their sudden *lapse* in security.

U.S. President Richard Nixon also visited in April, 1972, and this time Guy and I found ourselves sequestered on the roof of the Chateau Laurier Hotel which overlooks Parliament Hill. Long shifts were again the order of the day and our small, confined balcony provided a miserable observation post in the midst of the steady rain that consumed the capital. At the time both of us were taking night school courses at Carleton University and Guy was desperately attempting to study for a final exam, huddled in a darkened corner of the balcony.

It seemed a nondescript and uneventful duty until we learned sometime later that Arthur H. Bremer had been photographed in the crowd directly below our vantage point. It was Bremer who on May 15, 1972, just a month later, shot Alabama Governor George Wallace during his presidential campaign stop in Laurel, Maryland. Bremer had been stalking President Nixon but failed to find that opportunistic moment when he could carry out his plan. Perhaps it wasn't a wasted shift after all.

But political visits were not the only implications of life in the nation's capital. The lingering threats of the FLQ lingered in Ottawa like a bad dream. The FLQ was a Marxist revolutionary party that sought Quebec independence and resorted to violence to achieve its purpose. Responsible for more than two hundred bombings in Canada during the late 1960's which resulted in the deaths of at least five people, their vicious attacks came to a head in October 1970 with the kidnapping of British Trade Commissioner James Cross on October the 5th and five days later Quebec Labor Minister Pierre LaPorte.

The brazen kidnappings lead Quebec Premier Robert Bourassa to petition the Federal government for military assistance and Prime Minister Trudeau responded by invoking Canada's War Measures Act authorizing sweeping police powers and the military occupation of several Quebec cities. The next day the crises reached its apex when the FLQ assassinated LaPorte. Eventually, British Trade Commissioner James Cross was freed in exchange for the safe-conduct of his kidnappers to Cuba, but Paul Rose and the members of his terrorist cell were abandoned by their fellow FLQ compatriots to face charges for LaPorte's murder.

In this historical setting uneasy tensions surrounded the anniversary of the Cross and LaPorte kidnappings in October of 1971 and 1972, and when anonymous threats were made against Federal cabinet ministers and foreign diplomats our understudy training was again interrupted by our having to reinforce local police agencies in providing protection services. It was another round of flashlights, snub nose revolvers and midnight shifts.

35
The Real CSI

Today the popularity of a television series known as CSI, which stands for *Crime Scene Investigation,* leads people to believe that forensic scientists man the front lines in major police investigations sometimes even becoming involved in confrontations with dangerous criminals. But nothing could be further from the truth and while the work of the forensic scientist can enhance, corroborate and in some cases even solve a major crime, scenes of its practitioners dealing *personally* with the criminal element simply have no basis in reality. In the real world, major crime investigators handle the front line investigation, *technicians,* who are often specially trained police officers, collect evidence from crime scenes and deliver it to *forensic scientists* who work in the confines of a well-equipped laboratory. If a forensic scientist actually sees a person accused of a crime it's across the confines of a crowded courtroom and not in any face to face confrontation. For my part I was thankful that such frontline duties were a thing of the past. Life was too short and luck too limited.

My transfer to Ottawa and my acceptance into the RCMP's Forensic Laboratory signaled the beginning of a forensic career in document examination that would span the next thirty years – most of it in public service, but five years in private sector. My training as a expert in the identification of handwriting, signatures, forgeries, alterations, erasures, the decipherment of charred documents, the identification of counterfeit currency, the evaluation of typewriters, cheque writers and even the examination of marked playing cards and loaded dice lead to a labyrinth of incredibly interesting investigations ranging from frauds and forgeries to rape and murder.

But Ottawa is the Headquarters for the RCMP and its close proximity to the Federal government places additional stress on even the most grass roots investigations, a stress that is seldom felt in other parts of the country. When I arrived in Ottawa my commanding officer had told me that, if after my understudy training my heart was still in the West, the opportunity might be found for me to return. I thought it a strange comment at the time but after two years in the nation's capital I began to realize that even in the RCMP, at least in Ottawa, politics overshadowed police work.

When I rapped on the door of Superintendent Hedrick's office it was like he had been expecting me. A better officer you couldn't find. He was easy to talk to and man you could trust. He warmly invited me in and asked what was on my mind. And I said,

Well sir, I've finished my training. I came here to learn something that could help members in the field with their investigations, I've been here two years and to tell you the truth, I can't find a person in this city who cares one bit about the man in field or for that matter anything that happens west of the Ontario – Manitoba border. I know that there is a position coming open in Edmonton. I know that there are two French officers qualifying at the same time as me. I doubt you want to send either of them to the West. So I just want to tell you that if you want me to go – I'm ready.

He looked at me with a slight, knowing smile and he said,

You figured that out pretty well, but you don't know just how lucky you are, I'm from Brooks, Alberta and I've been trying to get back to the West for the last twenty years – I don't think I'll ever make it.

Two months later we were on our way to Edmonton and a position in the Document Section of the Forensic Laboratory.

36
Career in Chaos

With my understudy completed and my sour exposure with the political climate in Ottawa behind me I dove into the duties of my new position in earnest – and I loved it. Working in a section with three highly qualified examiners once again I felt I was contributing further to the cause of justice in our society. The infinite variety of casework created a level of job satisfaction I had not known since my front line detachment duties and work associates also became good friends. In fact, the entire forensic laboratory seemed like family and both professional and social life merged into one stressful yet satisfying element.

There was the case of a man who murdered his wife, put her outside on their apartment balcony in minus thirty degree weather until she froze solid, then proceeded to saw her body into a multitude of smaller pieces. After placing each piece in a separate garbage bags he drove the mountainous road from Jasper to Banff, Alberta, tossing bags at random over cliffs and into the rugged terrain. He then forged a government document stating that his wife had died in a motor vehicle accident, forged the minister of highways signature on it, and used it to drain her personal bank accounts in Holland.

Interestingly, he returned from Holland with a new wife who was present when the investigating officers removed traces of dried blood from the carpet of his apartment. His new spouse also believed his wife had died in an automobile accident. But what none of us knew until sometime later was that there had been several previous wives – whose current whereabouts could never be established.

There was the man who burned his wife to death in the back of their camper, the case of the deaf mute who bragged to bar patrons that he would like to know what it was like to rape and murder someone subsequently fulfilling his desire, a woman murdered in Spain, who had been an agent for Britain's secret service MI5 during WWII, a missing man in Russia, whom the communist government refused to produce, yet insisted was alive, producing forged documents in their attempt to receive, supposedly *on his behalf*, the half a million dollar inheritance awarded to him in North America. The cases were indeed endless and their variety easily kept boredom at bay. But the details, I suppose, are best left for another day perhaps even another book. For me it was enough to know that I could meaningfully contribute to the law enforcement community and be of assistance to my fellow officers who were still out there at the business end of the knife. It was truly a rewarding time.

Whoever coined the phrase *all good things must come to an end* probably never realized just how apropos it would be to so many people and in so many different situations. For me no sooner were things seemingly balanced and running like a well-oiled machine, then the bottom seemed to fall out. Perhaps the most significant of the changes that took place in our cohesive laboratory was the transfer of the officer in charge, and as employees in every walk of life can attest, the personality and priorities of the person in charge invariably sheds downward influencing and infecting the work ethic and morale of the staff below them, either positively or negatively. In the case of our replacement the change was not for the better.

Our new Inspector was surreptitiously known as "the old philosopher" and under his direction the laboratory staff suffered through a plethora of mandatory meetings that espoused everything from transactional analysis to transcendental meditation all intended, of course, to enhance, educate and enlighten what appeared to him to be the unwashed nature of the laboratory faculty. Sadly, at the same time, the *good Inspector* actually believed many of the strange concepts and philosophies he espoused, and while the staff privately doubted most hesitated to openly question the assorted views, tactics, mandates and conclusions of their appointed leader.

Sometimes I really wish I could bite my tongue, and keep my mouth shut, but it has never been a part of my natural makeup and when I see what I often refer to as plastic people, *command* and in some cases *demand,* obedience to that which is clearly out of step with reality, I have been known to open my mouth just long enough to change feet. It happened just that way the day I replaced our Section Head at a senior management meeting with the good Inspector.

It started out not unlike every other Section Head meeting with the supervisors of each science department and the administrative staff meeting with the Laboratory Manager to discuss business procedures and operations. But as was always the case with the *good Inspector* our twenty minute weekly agenda stretched to over an hour as he pontificated and shared with the group on another facet of his management philosophy. It was a meeting I was wishing my supervisor had not missed when the old philosopher made a statement that I could not overlook. He said,

You know I recently learned of a very interesting management tool that was recently employed by the Manitoba Telephones Company. It seems what they did was that they took all their junior managers, along with their wives or husbands, to a hotel for a week long management training seminar. During the week management sessions were held for their supervisors and various social functions were held in the evenings, but the real point of the seminar was not known until Friday morning when it was disclosed to the attendees that their hotel rooms had been electronically bugged. Then they played the tapes of the conversations that took place and people heard what others had said about them. Boy did it open up dialogue!

There was a look of astonishment on the faces that surrounded the table, but no one responded and then he continued,

Some people even found out that their spouses were not compatible with their careers. Some even got divorced! Maybe we should try something like that.

I was sitting immediately to his right. A fire burned within me, I couldn't hold back, and I said,

I'm sorry sir but that doesn't sound to me like good man management.

With a hint of displeasure in his voice he said,

What do you mean by that?

And I replied,

It sounds more like deceit. And furthermore, sir, I would just as soon that my wife was not compatible with my career so that I might actually have another voice to listen to when I get home at night.

He was visibly upset but he sloughed off my comments without further elaboration and abruptly adjourned the meeting. I didn't have to be a Rhodes Scholar to realize I hadn't exactly solidified a lifetime friendship.

Then, as I left the meeting one, of the other Section Heads, a woman, who would one day actually be appointed in Ottawa to oversee *Quality Assurance* for all the country's forensic laboratories, stopped me in the hallway, and whispered,

Boy, I sure agreed with what you said in there. I just couldn't believe what he was saying.

I gave her a rather blank look and asked,

Then why didn't you say something? Why didn't you back me up?

Well,

she said,

I really didn't want to get into it.

And then I rather rudely replied,

Pat, did you ever wonder how Adolph Hitler got into power in Germany? It was because one day people just like us sat around a table, just like that, and listened to him say, "Hey, I have a good idea let's kill all the Jews," and all the people around that table just sat there with crooked little smiles on their faces and thought – this guy is crazy! But not one of them opened their mouth to say anything in opposition, just like all of you did in there!

She apologized but it didn't help, the damage had been done. I had made the worst enemy of my career and he was just happened to be my superior officer.

I don't know how long the *good Inspector* stewed over my remarks, but it didn't take long for the repercussions to commence. Soon my Laboratory Reports, which provided the results of my examinations to the investigating officers, inexplicably sat on his desk for long periods of time before reluctantly being forwarded. Occasionally, he would bring one to my personal attention, in each case his intent seemed to be to reinforce some philosophic view which he assumed I needed to learn. In one such instance he drew my attention to the wording in a portion of one of my reports in which I had written,

The submission of additional specimen material may be beneficial to a further examination.

And he asked, *Why would you say "beneficial," why wouldn't you say it would be "efficacious?"*

To which I replied,

Sir, in my opinion, if an investigator has to pick up a dictionary to read my report than I haven't written it properly.

He retorted with,

If you write like that how do you ever expect them to believe we are scientists?

And he walked away.

I refused to rewrite it, he refused to forward it, and it sat on his desk for another six weeks before he grudgingly forwarded it on to the investigating officer. Of course his amateur antics had not kept me from telephoning the investigator and informing him verbally what the results of my examination had been and I'm sure he had either no idea or simply didn't care if his delay tactics adversely affected an investigation. Sadly, my struggles with him continued until the day he was promoted and transferred to Ottawa.

Interestingly, some ten years later, while driving to work one day, I heard the following news cast,

A long-standing lawsuit with past employees of Manitoba Telephones was settled yesterday in a Winnipeg courtroom. The suit arose over certain management techniques employed during the late 1970's when the company authorized electronic monitoring of hotel rooms to record the personal conversations of its employees. Details of the compensation packages were not disclosed.

It was nice to hear that some people did stand up for what they believed in.

37
Detour to the Right

I was always intensely devoted to the RCMP, considered a potential high-riser, a staff sergeant at fifteen years service. My name was even on a select list of those considered capable of greater things and yet somehow I perceived that my experience with the *good Inspector* had permanently damaged my career. The RCMP has deep roots originating in many of the old fashioned British military traditions where superior officers were never questioned and unswervingly obeyed; even those which might appear strangely misguided. Loyalty and obedience were mandatory and considered essential to any successful military action. I understood the code and I knew then that I could not expect to maintain even my own inadequate sense of moral values if I expected to rise to the heights. I would have to bite the bullet, learn to play the game, and keep my mouth shut, all of which I was woefully incapable of doing. It was at that moment that I grasped something which to me was even more hurtful, – I was Regimental Number 23706 – *I was just a number*.

It was inevitable, I suppose, that even after the *good Inspector* departed my time in the Force would be limited. The crises in my career had reached its apex and although I had experienced a number of life threatening situations in the past, the intensified emotional stress of the moment and seeming disintegration of my career brought me to my knees. The imbalance I had placed on the importance of my career over every other area of my life, including my family, drove me to the breaking point.

I would never have fashioned myself a candidate for suicide, yet, one dark night at three o'clock in the morning, in a state of deep emotional distress, I found myself seriously contemplating the issue. The importance I had placed on my career had selfishly overridden even the love for my family. It was then that I picked up the old Bible that had been given to me so many years before in that little Salvation Army church in the North end of Regina. I had trucked that Bible from pillar to post as something of a trophy for all those years and yet had never seriously considered its content or its message. I opened it and read the handwritten notation inside the front flyleaf. It simply read,

Behold the book whose leaves display Jesus, the truth, the light, and the way. Read it with diligence and prayer, search it and thou shalt find Him there.

I looked up from the page and silently prayed,

God, I'm going to read this book and if you're real you'd better show me, because if you're not real this is just another old history book and life is not worth living.

With the slowness of my reading skills it took a year to read that Bible from cover to cover, but I kept my promise, simultaneously beginning to dig into a study of the world's religions in general, assessing the tenants of Hinduism, Taoism, Buddhism, Confucianism and every other *ism* I could think of in an effort to see if any truth really existed. I arrived at one very clear conclusion – Christianity was different from all the rest. The others all seemed to say,

Do this – live this way – obeying our rules and regulations – and maybe – just maybe – we can't really be sure of course – but maybe – you'll make it into heaven, or at least our view of some equivalent state of being.

But Christianity said,

Jesus Christ is the Son of God. He died to pay for your sins upon the cross. Believe in Him with all your heart, all your soul and all your mind and your place in Heaven will be guaranteed; then go and live the way God would want you to live, not because you are required to, but because you want to, as an expression of your love and appreciation for what He has done on your behalf.

It seemed too simple, too easy, and yet the more thoroughly I dissected it, the more profound it became. Christianity simply overruled all others. My search was narrowed and the only hurdle that remained was to evaluate the denominational differences in Christianity which seemed so contradictory to the simplicity of the Bible's message.

I devoured books and searched libraries for answers to the questions that bothered me. What did Catholics believe that Protestants didn't? What about the Lutherans, Anglicans and Baptists and where did the Mormons fit into the equation? Slowly, but not surprisingly, God provided answers. By the time my initial year of study had concluded, I had accepted Jesus Christ as my personal Savior, been baptized, and begun attending church.

For me it was a serious time of evaluation, and God had proved more than capable of responding to my mid-night ultimatum. He opened the eyes of my understanding and allowed me to grasp the true meaning and value of life. He helped me to realize that the most important *things* in life – were not *things* at all, but *people* and *relationships.* Relationships not only with family and friends, but ultimately with Him. That's why I do not consider myself to have found *religion*, which can often be rigid, demanding and uncompromising, but a *relationship with God*, a loving Father, who knows everything about me, and loves me in spite of it.

38
Footsteps of Faith

Vince and Gladys Nelson, my wife's parents, lived in Regina. Vince had been a farmer during the depression era and, even though he supplemented his farming with work in the coal mines of Southern Alberta, ultimately, he was forced to consider other options. Since Vince could fix just about anything; he eventually developed an automotive business in the city of Regina.

Vince was a big, powerful man, but when he suffered a major heart attack at around sixty years of age, every family member believed he would die. Yet, Vince lived. Then one day, quite unexpectedly, his wife, Gladys was hospitalized and lapsed into a coma. By the time Gail and I arrived from Edmonton a large group of friends and family were already assembled at her beside. It was a vigil that continued all that night and throughout the next day.

At about five o'clock in the afternoon, the crowd departed for supper, leaving Gail and I alone at Gladys' bedside. Her breathing seemed heavy, labored and troubled. Gail sat at her bedside gently stroking her hand. Not quite knowing what else to do, I casually picked up the Gideon Bible I had found in the room opened it to the Book of Psalms. I walked over to the window and began to quietly read to myself. The verse that caught my eye virtually leapt from the page. It was as if I had been directed to a verse that was a perfectly scripted intercession to God on Gladys' behalf. The instant I read it – her labored breathing ceased – and she died. I was both shocked and amazed, yet strangely calm, as hospital staff suddenly appeared with a crash cart in a fruitless attempt to revive her. God had given us a crystal clear message of her acceptance and from that moment on I never doubted her salvation – though I had never spoken to her of her beliefs.

After all the confusion of the funeral and our return trip home I tried again to find that amazing verse. I searched every Psalm – line by line – it was not there. I thought, maybe I was mistaken, perhaps it was in the book of Proverbs, I searched again – still not there. Frustrated and bewildered, I telephoned an older Christian mentor, a man who had been a missionary in Papua New Guinea. I asked him if ever he had heard of a verse being read in the Bible that applied so specifically to a given situation and yet, afterward was simply not there. He said, *I believe I have.* Maybe that's why it's sometimes called the *living Word of God.*

It was the following summer when I finally summed the courage to share with my father-in-law the remarkable story of what took place the night Gladys died. He turned to me with an angry look and he said,

I don't want anything to do with a God who would take my wife. Don't ever speak to me about it again.

And I didn't. In fact, my wife and I simply made a vow to pray that he would not die until he had had every opportunity to accept the Lord Jesus as his Savior.

For Vince the heart attacks continued. On one such occasion, Gail's sister, Dolores, who was still living in Regina at the time, reported that the attending physician asked how long he had been an invalid to which she replied,

He's never been an invalid.

And the doctor said,

That's impossible; I've never seen a heart so scarred on anyone who was not an invalid. I wanted to do a bypass, but there is no place that I could possibly bypass to or from – well, he'll be an invalid from now on – he'll never leave this hospital.

Now, before this Vince had been living in a lakeside home at Kanata Valley on Long Lake near the city of Regina. His doctors had told him that even fishing was too strenuous for him so he had reluctantly sold his boat. But two weeks after this latest prognosis he left the hospital, threw away half of his pills, built himself a boat, and went fishing.

Remarkably, this type of thing continued for *twenty years.* Then, one day while I was at work, Gail called and told me that Dolores had phoned, her father had suffered another heart attack – but this time it was different – he wanted to speak to me. I left work immediately and drove straight from Edmonton to Regina, Gail would fly down later after she had arranged for the children. I arrived at 11 o'clock that night – Dolores and a friend were there with him and when he saw me he said,

Would you ladies please excuse me? I want to talk to Bob.

Then he looked a me with tears in his eyes and he said,

I want to go where Gladys is and I want you to tell me how to get there.

He confessed his sins and accepted Jesus Christ into his heart. A man – *a real man* – a man 84 years old and at that moment a new born babe in Christ. Then he asked me to apologize at his funeral to anyone he may have harmed during his lifetime. I shared a few verses of Scripture with him and retired to my parent's home to spend the night. When I arrived back at the hospital early the next morning Gail was already there. She said,

You know, the doctor just left, and when he came out from examining dad he asked, Was that your husband who spoke to him last night?

She went on,

I said Yes, it was.

And then he said,

Well, I don't know what he said to him, but today he is like a new man. It's like the weight of the world has been lifted off his shoulders.

Two weeks later, Vince Nelson left the hospital one more time and a short time later, at home, passed quietly into the presence of the Lord. Today – he's where Gladys is.

Many of my colleagues and former drinking buddies turned away from me when I openly professed my new-found faith in Christ. Some simply said,

Don't worry, he'll be back, it's just a faze.

Others were more openly critical and determined to watch my every step; predicting that I would soon embarrass myself and come back to my senses. One particular friend did not turn away, although he did tell me not to bother to share my beliefs with him anymore. He said, simply,

Well if it works for you fine, but it's not for me.

I left it at that and three years later he became a Christian following the example set by my wife, my mother, my father, my sister and several friends and relatives who also accepted Christ shortly after my conversion. For some, like my father and I, it was a radical change; sometimes slow in the process, but nonetheless very real.

Shortly after I became a Christian, I terminated my employment with the RCMP and since I was a qualified

document examiner I commenced a professional priv'
providing forensic document services to commerci.
communities. Not surprisingly, the cases were every bit a.
exhilarating. The use of forged documents to sell unregistered
bulls in Japan, an eighty-five million dollar law suit resulting
from a business being sold below market value, a doctor making
threats against nurses, bomb threats to oil companies and
numerous disputed Last Will and Testaments that pitted family
members against one another.

The most satisfying thing about my new- found schedule
flexibility was that it allowed me to commit 30-40 hours a week
in personal Bible study. My intention was – rather than to simply
accept what others said – to let the Bible speak for itself. After
all, if it really was God's word – who better to explain it? After
two years, I began to take correspondence courses from Emmaus
Bible School in Chicago, and later – in subjects like
Hermeneutics and Systematic Theology ultimately obtaining, a
Certificate in Christian Ministry, from Prairie Graduate school in
Calgary, AB.

I began receiving invitations to speak at various churches.
I conducted weddings and funerals. Even my approach to football
coaching changed. At the high school and Junior Football levels
Bibles were presented to graduating players – the team logo, the
player's name and jersey number were gold-leafed onto the front
cover – coaches' autographs were appended inside and the
statement I had found in my own presentation Bible was
appended on the inside flyleaf;

*Behold the book whose leaves display, Jesus the truth, the light,
the way. Read it with diligence and prayer, search it and thou
shalt find Him there.*

I remained in private practice for five years. Then, just as my
intense desire for private Bible study began to wane, I was
approached by the RCMP to ascertain any interest I might have in
returning to the Force. They were in need of my expertise and
would allow me to re-establish my pension benefits. I gratefully
accepted the offer and never regretted the opportunity to serve the

additional fifteen years which allowed me to retire in 1999 after thirty years of service from the Force I loved and respected.

Although life has not been necessarily easier since I became a believer – I have, nonetheless, found God faithful through every trial and hardship. Having put one's hand to the plow there is simply no turning back – nor any desire to do so. Sadly, I did not become a Christian until I was thirty-three years of age. There is a line from a song by a lady named *Marijohn* that has always haunted me – it says,

I wasted more years than we let Jesus live down here.

I became a Christian at 33 years of age, the same age Jesus was when we crucified Him – but by God's grace I've now broken even.

39
What is Truth?

My five year hiatus from the RCMP was a badly needed pit stop in life; an opportunity to turn aside from the hustle and bustle that consumed my days and converted them into so many seemingly meaningless years. It was a chance to slow down long enough to think – to *muse* on the ultimate purpose of life's race and my place within it, to wrestle with ultimate questions and struggle to comprehend truth.

Isn't it strange that some words in the English language seem to fall out of favor over time? *Muse* is one of those words. We don't hear it used much these days, perhaps because it expresses the idea of entering *into a state of deep thought* on some issue, which is clearly not a proactive pastime in our post modern *enlightened* age. Or, perhaps it's just that the torrid pace of life today seems to deny any unobstructed opportunity to just *stop and think*.

It's also interesting that in the English language when the letter *"a"* is placed in front of a word it often changes the meaning of that word to the exact opposite. For example, if something is said to be *atypical* it becomes the complete opposite to that which is said to be *typical*. Now if we apply that logic to the word *muse* we have *amuse* from which the word - *amusement*, is derived. In fact, *amusement* is clearly intended to entertain us without our having to tax ourselves by thinking too deeply. The simple philosophy is, sit back, relax, and we will *amuse* you. And, so not surprisingly, even when a short pit stop can be found in the rat race of life, most of us would rather be *amused* than use that time to *muse* over any particular issue. Unfortunately, there is no getting around the fact that in order understand the Bible, one must apply themselves to it – God will not simply open our heads and pour in knowledge. He expects us to think – to *muse* for ourselves.

During WWII Winston Churchill is said to have spoken to a group of striking British coalminers who were concerned about the value of their contribution to the war effort. In responding to their concerns Churchill likened their efforts to those fighting directly on the front lines. Then he said something like this,

One day, when this war is over and your children and your children's children ask you what you did in the war, you may proudly say – "We won the coal!"

Remarkably, the translators of the Authorized King James version of the Bible, used this same word to describe what the Apostle Paul was trying to portray to First Century Christians concerning the earnestness with which he addressed the Christian life. His desire was to *win Christ,* a victory that could only be gained in the same manner as those who dug for coal in Britain, with rolled up sleeves, bent backs and the sweat of the brow. Coal miners hammer, claw, chip and scratch to loose the valuable coal from its bed of solid rock, and by extension, that's exactly what God expects of those who would understand the deeper things of God more fully. They must apply themselves earnestly to the task in order to gain the fullness of its message. They are to *win Christ* just as coalminers *win the coal.* God expects each one of us to think for ourselves.

Unfortunately, many in our society refuse to apply themselves to discovering truth. In fact, many today simply argue that there is no such thing as *truth* – that all truth is merely *relative*, that what is true for you is not necessarily true for me. Ironically, this post modern creed is an illusion in itself, seemingly intended to sanitize and massage truth into something more palatable for those who refuse to grapple with life's deeper metaphysical issues. Issues like *meaning* and *purpose*, the existence of a higher power, and one's *answerability* and ultimate *accountability* to that power. Not surprisingly then, truth becomes more of a search for what is *personally approved* than what can be *objectively understood*.

Yet, even common sense dictates that two totally opposite conclusions cannot both be right, although they obviously can both be wrong. Polar opposites cannot both be true unless one is a further understanding of the other. For example; the long standing principle that *what goes up must come down* is as true today as it was when when Newton sat beneath the apple tree. Of course, we also know today, that *what goes up must come down unless it goes up far enough that it goes into orbit.* But, even that progressive revelation does not negate the law of gravity. It simply extends our understanding of it.

Unfortunately, *common sense* is no longer a *common quality* in society. Indeed, some people firmly believe that to be open minded one must never come to a definitive belief in anything – a sad fact that was illustrated to me by one of my Commanding Officers who once said to me,

You know the trouble with you Christians is you're neither objective nor open-minded.

To which I replied,

Well sir, my idea of being objective is to approach a subject without predetermining what I'm going to believe about it. However, when I discover the truth of it, I grasp onto it, and never let it go. You seem to think being objective is never having to believe in anything and that an open mind is having a mind like a sewer pipe where ideas simply flow in one end and out the other and where conclusions are never drawn on anything.

I regretted the sharpness of my reply, but when I was later promoted on this officer's personal recommendation, I knew he had not allowed our differences of opinion to affect his approval of the work I was doing. He stood in marked contrast to the *good inspector*, who had so jeopardized my earlier career.

It never ceases to amaze me how so many, otherwise intelligent people, buy into the philosophies and unchallenged values of today's society. Many accept such things as *political correctness* and the *Theory of Evolution*, without ever having seriously evaluated the evidence for themselves; not only readily accepting those claims from supposed professionals and scientists, but even extending such credibility to sport figures and a variety of other celebrities. It reminds me of a line from a song B.J. Thomas song that says,

It's easier to sell a lie than give the truth away.

That statement was never more true than it is today. George Orwell probably never realized how prophetic he was when he wrote,

In a time of universal deceit, telling the truth becomes a revolutionary act.

Indeed, the plain truth is right before our eyes – if only we'll take the time to think for ourselves.

The Bible records how the Roman Procurator, Pontius Pilate, stood before Jesus and facetiously asked, *What is truth?* Then, he simply turned and walked away. He came face to face with the One who claimed to be *the truth,* yet couldn't pause long enough to entertain an answer to his own question. Sadly, Pilate epitomizes many today, who mistakenly assume that peer pressure, social obligations and the general busyness of life somehow exempt them from the necessity of having to stop and think – to *muse about life itself.* Not surprisingly, history records that Pontius Pilate later fell into disfavor with his superiors during the reign of the Roman Emperor Caligula and subsequently committed suicide,

– A life without meaning has no value even in the eyes of the one who possess it.

Pilate was a lot like me – driven to succeed, a potential high-riser, who suddenly became conscious of the fact that he was little more than a small spoke in a much larger wheel, a wheel that wouldn't lose a single revolution at the loss of one insignificant spoke. Fortunately for me, unlike Pilate, I did not turn and walk away from the truth. Notwithstanding the influences of political correctness, peer pressure and the unsubstantiated theories of so-called, science, in the final assessment it doesn't matter what other people think about us – only what God thinks. He has obligated each one of us to reach our own conclusions. My search brought me to the realization that life itself confirms the existence of many elemental truths that manifest themselves in a variety of life-challenging and hopefully life-changing ways. For example,

The truth is that organizations don't care about people – people care about people.

The truth is that there is a very fine line between living and dying – and while some choose to terminate life early, there are multitudes who value it dearly and wish they could live just one more day.

The truth is that life does not boil down to satisfying career aspirations, rising to positions of power or prestige – nor is it about the accumulation of things. Contrary to the bumper sticker which proclaims, *The person who dies with the most toys wins* – they not only do not win, but become some of life's biggest losers. The truth is that the most important things in life are not *things* at all – but intangibles like *family*, *love* and *relationships*. If you don't believe me read the biography of Howard Hughes.

The truth is that man did not descend from an ape but through the special creation of God. Micro evolution exists and is provable – macro evolution is neither. The current popular theory of evolution is simply a fairy tale for adults.

The truth is that we are not here to see through each other so much as to see each other through.

The truth is that religion can be distorted into an obsession and history is littered with the carnage of its bad examples, yet, a right relationship with God can provide hope and peace in the midst of the most violent storms that assail our lives.

The truth is that those who believe in nothing often fall for anything.

The truth is we will not be judged on what others think about us. We will be judged on what God thinks of us.

The truth is that God wants men – but He doesn't need them. Men need God – but don't want Him.

Truth is that there is a physical realm and there is a spiritual realm. We perceive the physical to be *reality* and the spiritual we vaguely assume is but a *shadow.* The truth is that one day the physical will seem to have been the shadow and the spiritual an eternal reality.

I once had an old friend ask me what I expected to get out of all this study and introspection. All I could think of to say was,

Well, how about eternal life?

To which he replied,

Eternal life, who cares about eternal life? I don't care one bit what happens to me after I die.

As far as I know, he has never come to believe in life after death. He sold out to a system that teaches a worldview that crushes hope and refutes moral values. A system that espouses physical life as all there is and in the process denies its adherents any hope for the future. Is it any wonder that such a worldview allows a man to take another's life without the slightest hint of remorse? If one believes man is no different than an animal, then subsequently, taking a human life is really of no more consequence than stepping on an ant. What a tragic belief system to force-feed to our children and grandchildren all the while disguising it in a magician's cloak called *scientific truth*. As for me, I have come to believe that man was created by God – is special – precious in His sight – and made in His image. I believe that each of us will ultimately answer not only for our beliefs, but also for our actions.

The truth is that trusting Jesus Christ as your Savior is the most important decision you will ever make – nothing else even comes close, or has such eternal implications. It's the final answer in life's test. God deals with each one of us on a personal, individual basis. His love and forgiveness are available to all – and absolutely free. It seems too simple to be true; but it's exactly that simplicity that keeps us from grasping the most important truth that life has to offer.

Today Christianity receives a bad rap, not only from its enemies, but also because it has been *wounded in the house of its friends*. The arrogance of organized religion, is just as hypocritical today as it was when Jesus walked this earth. The misguided assertions of science, our misdirected love of money, materialism, personal and professional pride, and Biblical ignorance have combined to twist and distort God's simple message of love and forgiveness. As a result, *true Christianity* has often been hidden behind a veil of innuendo, insults and half-truths. Dr. Leslie D. Weatherhead was right when he said,

The trouble with some of us is that we have been inoculated with small doses of Christianity which keeps us from catching the real thing.

The truth is that Christianity has not failed; it has never seriously been tried.

40
Bonus Time

I retired from the RCMP after thirty years of service, satisfied that I had done what I could to contribute to the administration of justice in the country that I love. I'm proud of those I served with at every stage of my career and I am still convinced that many of those serving in the police forces of our nation today are doing so with honorable intentions; seeking to stem what seems to be a rising tide of crime and violence in our land.

I am not as equally persuaded, however, that the justice and political systems share in that commitment. Today victim's rights are virtually non-existent, while the rights of criminals are badly over emphasized. Victims, who desperately need compassion and, in some cases, compensation, are quickly forgotten while criminals are provided with publicly funded attorneys and, even if convicted, sent to facilities that cater to their every whim. This country does not have a *justice system* but a *legal system*. But justice *delayed* in not necessarily *justice denied* and one day God will judge those who have eluded the efforts of police officers and the court system.

A new prison opened not long ago in Grande Prairie, Alberta, boasted an outstanding Mountain View and surprisingly high standard of living. When a group of senior citizens was taken on a tour of the facility one elderly man openly began to weep. When asked what was wrong he told the tour guide it was because he knew of so many seniors living far below this standard of living in his own community. No one suggests treating criminals poorly. However, when honest law-abiding citizens, who have spent their lives contributing positively to a country, are living below the standards afforded to those that society must incarcerate, something is dreadfully wrong.

Theories of crime and rehabilitation will always fail when punishment is purposefully neglected. Remarkably, God himself provided us with the greatest example of justice in human history when Jesus Christ was crucified at Calvary. The crime of sin had been committed. God's law declared that the punishment for sin was death and Jesus bore that punishment on our behalf. The crime had been committed; the law had been violated and the punishment had been dealt. When Jesus Christ rose from the dead God's offer of forgiveness and mankind's rehabilitation could commence. Subsequently, God brings each one of us to a point in our lives where we must recognize our guilt and gratefully accept His Son's suffering on our behalf. Only then can our lives be renewed and true rehabilitation begin.

I am thankful today that God spoke to me in the wee small hours of that morning so many years ago – at a time when life seemed no longer worth living, when truly selfish notions corrupted and distorted my vision causing me to overlook the deep abiding love of those closest to me. How self-centered and thoughtless the act of suicide really demonstrates itself to be when one stops to consider its impact upon those who love them. It surely is a *permanent solution* to a *temporary problem.* There is no life, no matter how seemingly hopeless the possessor believes it to be, that is not worth living. God can rehabilitate and reshape any life into something that brings blessing to others and glory to Himself. Life is God's precious gift to each one of us and must be handled with the utmost care.

Strange, isn't it, how one day we find that God is not as invisible or as distant as we once thought Him to be. Then, as we begin to reassess the events that have shaped our lives we slowly begin to grasp how it was God all the while, weaving the circumstances of life to form our own unique tapestry. A spider's web of time and chance, destined to draw us to that place where we could finally come to an end of *self* and a new beginning with Him. A place where we would no longer feel constrained, controlled or confined by the world's interpretation of success or its sad misconception of *the good life*. A place where true beauty, worth and value come into sharp focus. Where life is worth living, and where all things become new.

Now, as I enter the latter years of life, my goals and priorities have changed. The center of my life is no longer *me* but *Him*. My life's purpose has become a commitment to *worship God* and *serve others*. I am pleased when the opportunity presents itself to speak on His behalf, to share my love of music by entertaining at senior's centers and care facilities, or by writing books such as this one, which may, I hope, cause someone to stop and ponder the real essentials of life.

I have come to understand that a *Christian* is not someone who *does not sin,* but someone who recognizes that *they are a sinner.* Yet, while I fail God everyday, I know that he is a loving and forgiving Father. I no longer strive to be *the best,* but merely seek to make the best out of what God made me be – *just being me* and I look forward to the future – because that's where I'm going to spend the rest of my life. I don't believe that God created this entire Universe without an eternal purpose and I'm looking forward to being part of that great plan. Now, as I move through the remainder of my life I want to take the advice offered by Minnie Louise Haskins when she wrote,

I said to the man who stood at the gate of the year. "Give me a light that I may tread safely into the unknown." and he replied, "Go out into the darkness and put your hand into the hand of God. That shall be to you better than light and safer than a known way."

My life, at least to this point in time, has been somewhat of an adventure; not along a road I might personally have chosen to travel – but a road by which God led me to life's ultimate crossroads. A place where I could finally come to appreciate the intrinsic value of this fleeting thing we so casually call *life*. At times the journey seemed laboriously slow, as during my teenage years when impatience overwhelmed me, or during mid-life struggles when the routine and monotony of the grind made life seem just so *daily*. Yet, as I scan back over the years, it has all flashed by in nothing more than the *twinkling of an eye*.

Life is God's testing ground, the place where the models He has designed can be put through their paces, where their performances can be evaluated as they encounter ruts and rigors along the road of life. Yet, in a very real sense, God's intention has always been that every model should one day recognize its own inherent unreliability and return to its maker for the necessary modifications and repairs. Eternity lies just beyond the horizon and each of us will finish life's journey *alone*. Just as I once awoke on a cold dark street, deserted by my friends, and could no longer take the short cut across the railroad tracks – each one of us will one day find ourselves *taking the long way home*.

Robert A. Dolman

Bob Dolman is a retired police officer and Forensic Scientist who's rich and engaging storytelling style has made him a popular public speaking figure.

His thirty year career in the RCMP began with postings in Revelstoke and Kamloops and culminated with service as a Document Examiner in the RCMP laboratories in Ottawa and Edmonton. As a member of the *Canadian Society of Forensic Science* and the *American Board of Forensic Document Examiners* his training as an expert in a multitude of forensic examinations led to his participation in a wide variety of criminal and civil investigations ranging from forgery to murder.

In 1968 Bob received the RCMP Commanding Officer's Commendation for Bravery in Kamloops, B.C.

"In the capture of an armed and dangerous man who had fired at members of the Force."

Bob has always been active in his community and a passionate supporter of minor league football. He personally coached football in four different provinces over a twenty-five year period. Bob was recognized by Kamloops NL Radio as the *"Good Guy of the Day"* in 1971 and Edmonton's CFRN Television as the *Sportsman of the Week"* in 1977. He was named football *"Coach of the Year"* on five occasions and *Alberta's Provincial Amateur Coach of the Year* in 1986. He was nominated for the *Alberta Sports Council Award* in 1987 and *Citizen of the Year* awards in Sherwood Park, Alberta in 1984 and 1986. In 1988 Bob received a special invitation to coach with the Edmonton Eskimos, of the Canadian Football League, in the league's All-Star Game.

Since he became a Christian in 1977 Bob has extended his public speaking to include both teaching and preaching at a variety of churches including, Baptist, Pentecostal, Nazarene, Alliance, Lutheran and Christian Brethren Assemblies. He completed a Certificate in Christian Ministry from Prairie Graduate School in Calgary, Alberta in 1999.

Bob was nominated for the Order of Canada 1987, was the keynote speaker at the National Student Conference in 1988 and most recently the quest speaker at the Langley's Leadership Prayer Breakfast in 2009.

Since his retirement from the RCMP in 1999 Bob has spent his time in writing, furthering his studies, and entertaining seniors by singing his favorite country and western tunes. This is Bob's third book, the others being, *How Does Your Garden Grow* (on spiritual growth) and *Speaking for the Master* (on public speaking in churches). Both titles, together with several music CD's are available on line at Lulu.com.

Bob and his wife Gail moved to Langley, British Columbia in 2007 where they attend North Langley Community Church. They have two children and five grandchildren.